BASICS
GRAPHIC DESIGN

03

Gavin Ambrose

Idea
Generation

Ethical: aware-
ness/
reflect-
ion/
debate

academia

An AVA Book

Published by AVA Publishing SA
Rue des Fontenailles 16
Case Postale
1000 Lausanne 6
Switzerland
Tel: +41 786 005 109
Email: enquiries@avabooks.com

Distributed by Thames & Hudson (ex-North America)
181a High Holborn
London WC1V 7QX
United Kingdom
Tel: +44 20 7845 5000
Fax: +44 20 7845 5055
Email: sales@thameshudson.co.uk
www.thamesandhudson.com

Distributed in the USA & Canada by:
Ingram Publisher Services Inc.
1 Ingram Blvd.
La Vergne TN 37086
USA
Tel: +1 866 400 5351
Fax: +1 800 838 1149
Email: customer.service@ingrampublisherservices.com

English Language Support Office
AVA Publishing (UK) Ltd.
Tel: +44 1903 204 455
Email: enquiries@avabooks.com

© AVA Publishing SA 2013

ISBN 978-2-940411-81-8

Library of Congress Cataloguing-in-Publication Data
Leonard, Neil; Ambrose, Gavin.
Basics Graphic Design 03: Idea Generation /
Neil Leonard, Gavin Ambrose p. cm.
Includes bibliographical references and index.
ISBN: 9782940411818 (pbk. :alk. paper)
eISBN: 9782940447428
1. Graphic design (Typography) 2. Creative thinking
Z246 .L456 2012

10 9 8 7 6 5 4 3 2 1

Design by Gavin Ambrose
Cover image by Vesna Pešić BECHA @Machas
and Sushi

Production by AVA Book Production Pte. Ltd., Singapore
Tel: +65 6334 8173
Fax: +65 6259 9830
Email: production@avabooks.com.sg

0.1
Moving card
Dowling Duncan

The simplest solutions are often the
most effective. This moving card
for a couple with the surname Bird,
uses the icon of a birdhouse. Their
move – from the city of London, UK,
to the rural county of Kent – is visually
represented through the change from
brick to weather-boarding, reflecting
the local building materials used in the
different locations. The two birdhouses
also represent the arrows of the
'This way up' symbol, referencing
packaging and moving.

The Birds have moved from a house in south London to a cosy barn in Kent

Contents

Good design begins with good ideas, generated in response to a given design brief. Successful visual outcomes can only be facilitated by the generation of great ideas, driven by research that will ultimately provide you with a range of potential design solutions. This book explores the different ways in which the designer can generate ideas.

There are many levels of idea generation, from macro to micro; from brainstorming to more focused, selective and strategic systems. Creative thinking is a skill that can be developed. This book explores a variety of approaches, theories and strategies that will help you to do this.

Graphic designers have used various techniques and strategies over the years that engender a wide range of new and innovative ideas and design solutions. A selection of some of those more historically situated strategies are explained, and related practical exercises encourage you to explore them in relation to your own design work.

This book also introduces some critical thinking based on the writing of authors, as well as pieces by great designers. It covers more abstract ideas concerned with idea generation as well as offering practical examples, strategies, case studies and exercises.

Ideas are the basis of good design. Generating, selecting and developing those ideas will be fundamental to you as a practising graphic designer. This book will help you get started and generate more ideas and a range of interesting, effective and relevant design solutions.

0.2
Alternative
The Creative Method

In crowded or saturated markets, you need to work hard to make a product stand out. A really strong idea can create the product's unique selling point (USP). The brief for this packaging for a premium organic wine was to produce something that would be a true talking point – something that could not be missed. Playing on the product's organic nature, the name 'Alternative' reflects a new way of looking at organic packaging. Every aspect of the packaging was organic – from the laser-cut balsa wood, to the string and wax used to fix the label to the bottle, and even the inks used to print the image.

0.2

Chapter 1 – Basic principles

This chapter will help you understand the basic principles that can be used to start to generate ideas. Simple exercises that can be undertaken as an individual or as part of a group will help you get to grips with the basics of idea generation.

The processes are presented in clear and practical ways so that you will quickly be able to incorporate them into your project work. To help you further, these examples are backed up by activities that explore their use in educational and work-based environments. These activities will form the building blocks for the more challenging ideas that we will look at in later chapters.

There are a few ways that you can prepare, prior to undertaking idea generation activities and techniques, to ensure that you get the best from these activities. If you think of the design process as a journey, and ideas as the things you see along the way, some initial thoughts regarding the route you will take will help you map your way.

In terms of a design project, whether you are a student or a professional, the most important thing you should get to grips with is the brief. The brief is a vital tool that should indicate what you need to create, where it will go and who will use it – effective idea generation will help you achieve this. You should not restrict yourself too heavily and should be open to exploring all lines of enquiry.

As your ideas progress, you should constantly refer back to the brief and consider whether the work you are doing is helping you to move forwards. Whilst it is good to take the time to fully explore your ideas, you have to understand the parameters of your project. This is especially true when a client is paying for your time; they will want you to explore and discover innovative solutions, but also to be accountable and stay reasonably on track.

Once you have familiarized yourself with the brief, start making things! Start anywhere within your project; a new project can seem like a mammoth undertaking, so try to find one part that inspires you and work from there. This book will encourage you to challenge your assumptions and break your normal patterns so that you can achieve work that goes far beyond your expectations.

1.1
Oxford Brookes University
Hat-trick Design

Oxford Brookes University, a leading learning and teaching institution in the UK, commissioned a series of environmental graphics for use during the regeneration of the university campus. The graphics appear on hoardings, in print and as sculptures around the campus. The simple icon creates an effective metaphor for the activities of the university, as Hat-trick explain: 'The initiative employs an icon of learning and growth – the tree – to communicate these achievements. Each tree was created individually, showing the diversity and breadth of the university. The use of the tree also draws a parallel to the leafy nature of this Oxford campus, as well as the idea of setting down roots and establishing them for future generations. The scheme will run concurrently with the regeneration work at the campus and a collection of over 150 varieties of tree will be created in various guises.'

Tip #1 – Just start

It is easy to use limitations as an obstacle for not starting a project. Pick one aspect, set a time limit (for example, one hour) and work, then abondon it; take a break, and pick another section to attack.

Hungry for change

Obesity and malnutrition might seem problems that are worlds apart. But undergraduates who study Applied Human Nutrition at Brookes look at both ends of the scale – and learn to think about dietary issues as a truly global phenomenon.

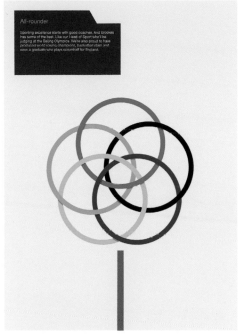

All-rounder

Sporting excellence starts with good coaches. And Brookes has some of the best. Like our Head of Sport who'll be judging at the Beijing Olympics. We're also proud to have produced world rowing champions, basketball stars and even a graduate who plays scrum-half for England.

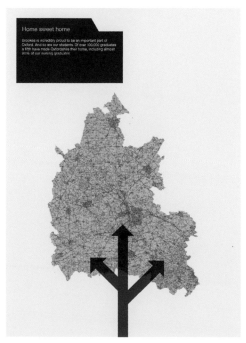

Home sweet home

Brookes is incredibly proud to be an important part of Oxford. And so are our students. Of over 100,000 graduates a fifth have made Oxfordshire their home, including almost 80% of our nursing graduates.

Engine of the future

Our students are pioneering the development of hybrid racing engines which will compete at the same level as gas guzzling conventional engines. We've even secured sponsorship to give them the best possible facilities.

1.1

Creative environment

The place in which you work should be conducive to creative practice. Everybody works in different ways – some prefer clean spaces, and some prefer organized chaos. However this area is ordered, it should contain the things that will help you move forwards – tools to draw with, magazines, books, an Internet connection and refreshments. If all of these are close at hand there should be no reason for you to interrupt the creative flow.

To work effectively for a sustained period of time, you should look to keep noise and distractions to a minimum. This includes answering emails. The ability to immerse yourself in design problems is key, and this takes time. To create effective solutions you should know everything about the project you possibly can, so be prepared to research the client, context and market thoroughly. Having the space and means to do this effectively is key, so however you work (files on a computer, folders and sketchbooks, or pin boards), make sure each project is kept together and is distinguishable from the others – bad organization could cause you to lose hours of work.

1.2—1.4
Corporate identity development
Dowling Duncan

Creating environments and situations that facilitate creativity is an important part of the design process. Here, Dowling Duncan have displayed a wide selection of artwork by Noma Bar for their client, San Francisco-based law firm Coblentz, Patch, Duffy & Bass, to choose from for their new corporate identity. Engaging with the client in this way includes them in a process they may not usually be exposed to.

1.2

Tip #2 – Listen to baroque music

Studies have shown that listening to baroque music, such as Vivaldi's The Four Seasons, increases alpha activity in the brain, which is associated with creativity. If music helps you think (or un-think), then so be it. Generating the right environment will help creativity, either by focusing your mind, or by allowing you to forget.

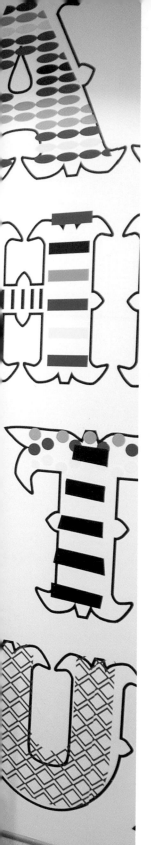

1.5—1.6
The creative environment
Studio Myerscough

Being in an environment that is conducive to creative thinking can make a real difference to the idea generation process.

I am lucky to have a few spaces to work in. I keep this space as a blank canvas, white walls with wonderful top light, with only a table and a few chairs. So when I want to make something I can start straight away. The space is temporarily taken over by the particular project and as soon as the project is complete everything is taken off the walls and cleared away ready for a new project to start at any time.

Morag Myerscough

1.6

Distraction

Ideas come hard when a person's mind is cluttered, no matter how they like to work. Distraction and a change of atmosphere can sometimes open the mind to new ideas. When you are struggling to find ideas, the best thing is to get out of the studio and go for a walk. Everyone knows a quiet place where they can get some peace and relax, be it a park, the beach or a coffee shop – once you've relaxed, your mind will refocus and you will be able to think more clearly.

Most designers find the best ideas occur when they are thinking about other things – often in the most everyday places, such as over the breakfast table or on their way to work. This happens because the mind is relaxed, uncluttered and not working too hard on the tasks it is engaged in. It is not the best idea to rely on this intervention (especially when there is a deadline looming), but clearing the decks can sometimes be as effective as any other idea generation process.

1.7—1.8
The Complete Harry Potter Collection
Webb & Webb

When Webb & Webb were asked to design a box set for the Harry Potter book series, they had an unusual brief – not to reference the films. Due to copyright issues, the film style and imagery could not be used, so a new style had to be developed.

The designers used an intriguing mechanism to develop the packaging for the collection – asking the hypothetical question, 'If Harry Potter was sent these books, how would they arrive?'. From this starting point, the design took on a life of its own, separate to, but still reminiscent of, the films. The resulting packaging features a series of trompe l'oeil (see page 70) effects, and fictional details such as the 'Owl Post' delivery stamp.

1.7

  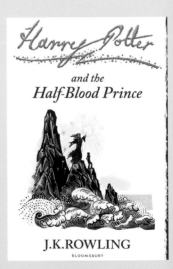

1.8

Be inspired and be informed

When working on a tough project, being inspired is half the battle. Inspiration will partly come from the brief, but the rest has to come from you. A graphic designer should have a very good overview of recent developments within their industry and know the latest trends, technologies and talents. This will not just feed into your work, but will also make you more aware of the current possibilities within the discipline, and more knowledgeable about where things might go next. This knowledge can be gained through a general overview of the arts, politics and of culture as a whole, as each is dependent on the other.

The colours used in the most recent fashion shows can indicate trendy and relevant choices, whereas an overview of economics may help you find jobs and materials in growing sectors. Look at contemporary and historical examples of design – try not to be too narrow as tastes and ideas change, but they are always influenced by what has come before. Good blogs and publications should provide you with lots of examples of projects that could be similar to yours. You should look beyond the context of the work and consider any elements that might benefit you, such as typographic styling, colour palettes and materials.

Inspiration can grab you at any point so being prepared to record it will help you progress projects with greater ease. In addition to this, you may happen upon things that inspire you and give you ideas purely by chance. Therefore it is wise to carry a sketchbook, pen and camera with you at all times to avoid losing these unexpected insights. You cannot expect to be inspired by simply sitting in a studio. Design is a lifestyle – ideas and inspiration can come to you at any point and should never be disregarded.

1.9

1.9—1.10
Sushi **Issue 13**
Vesna Pešic BECHA

Taking inspiration from the theme of 'labyrinth', Vesna created this striking and thought-provoking magazine cover. The aesthetics and the simplicity of the idea help make this such a successful design.

Tip #3 – Look, listen and collect

Spending time looking, listening and collecting will inform your ideas and design practice. 'If you stuff yourself full of poems, essays, plays, stories, novels, music, you automatically explode every morning like Old Faithful.' – Ray Bradbury

1.10

This commission reminded me of the complexity of the human mind. The illustration represents the birth of an idea.

Vesna Pešić BECHA

Context

The context of your work is the place it will exist once it is completed. This might be a physical place if you are designing packaging or advertising, it may also appear in film, online, or in an interactive environment. The context for your work will normally be indicated in the brief, and this can be the starting point for many ideas.

A firm understanding of where you are going with a project will suggest many ideas straight away, and amongst these you will find possible resolutions. Understanding where the finished work will exist may also suggest materials you could use. For example, if your designs are going to be placed outside they will need to be durable, but if they are going to be sold as luxury items the construction should reflect this.

Exploring the context will also suggest whether an idea is worth pursuing. If it is immediately clear that your idea will not lead you towards a suitable outcome, it is not worth following up; however, you should record every idea, as projects change and develop so initially rejected concepts may be more suitable at a later point.

Point of difference
Something that differentiates your product from the competition. This is particularly important in crowded markets, such as food packaging.

Personification
The attribution of a personal nature or human characteristics to something that is not human.

1.11—1.12
Krc&Ko
Peter Gregson Studio

Krc&Ko. (Crunch&Co. in English) is a line of snack products with packaging designed by Peter Gregson Studio. The design of this new product involved entering a new market, which required a distinct point of difference. In order to achieve this, the designers have personified the brand into a series of animated characters.

1.11

1.12

Whether you are working alone or as part of a group, it is a good idea to map preliminary ideas on paper as a means of getting something down quickly that affirms the aims of the project and acts as a base for further activity. By noting key words and looking for links and associations, the very action of writing can help develop new ideas.

These paper-based idea generation sessions work best when they are fast-paced and there are no limits imposed on the thoughts noted. If conducted this way, these activities can really push the limits of current thinking and inform original and innovative concepts.

Spider diagrams

A spider diagram can be seen as a primitive technique, but it can allow you to reach concepts far beyond those you might initially come up with. The technique is similar to mind mapping (see page 24), but is generally less formal and is best undertaken as a short, snappy exercise. It is a good way to get a lot of ideas on the page in a short period of time and can help you to generate some exciting concepts.

An effective spider diagram is simple – write what you are trying to achieve in the centre of a page and then give it 'legs'. Each time you add a new section to your diagram you should explore this and begin to give it legs of its own. Consider each element separately, thinking about options and the execution of it outside of your initial objective.

1.13
Spider diagram
A spider diagram allows you to rapidly explore multiple ideas. By exploring a series of sub-topics, options can be considered that would normally be discounted.

Tip #4 – Spider diagrams

• Look for associations, not hard facts.

• Try exploring one aspect until it is exhausted.

• Once several areas are mapped, look for common elements.

• Use short terms and phrases.

• Work fast!

This will help you to consider ideas that you would not otherwise have had. You can also draw links between the legs of your diagram – this will likely make it look like a spider's web.

The first few sections of your spider diagram will usually consist of ideas that seem fairly obvious, but the further outwards you move, the more extreme and unusual they become. The outer legs can then be explored in different combinations. Taking strands that are not immediately connected and considering what they might mean together will provide more innovative solutions.

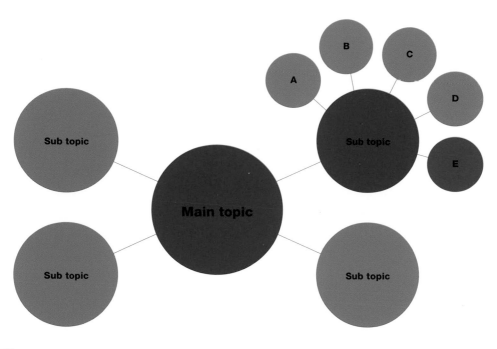

1.13

Mind mapping

Developed by author and educator Tony Buzan, mind mapping is another good way to get a wide range of thoughts onto paper quickly. Building on the idea of the spider diagram (see page 22), a mind map adds structure and visuals making this a process of finding links in a determined way, as opposed to making quick assumptions.

By drawing lines between a number of concepts and ideas, a focus and route forwards can be found. It can be used as a way to generate new ideas, or to help visualize and structure your existing thoughts.

Mind maps can be text based, or include drawings, clippings and photographs. Interactive technologies and websites now make it possible to add sound and video. Normally a mind map will start by writing down a phrase, word or image that describes the design problem that you are trying to address. Elements that relate directly to this starting point are then added, creating a second tier of information. Once this level has been explored you can begin to consider things that relate to it, creating a third level of information. As this progresses and more levels are added, the concepts explored will relate less to the initial focus and begin to suggest new avenues of enquiry. Throughout this activity it is useful to draw lines between the pieces and areas that relate to one another, as this will help track backwards later on. From here you can start to compare ideas and concepts and you will discover interesting relationships.

To ensure your mind map is effective and easy to read, you should think about how to differentiate the sections. As you begin new sections, it will help legibility if you alter the colours of the lines and text. Consider how you will indicate the areas that you feel might be key to your investigation later on; good ways of doing this are varying the style and size of text, or the colour. In this respect it works as a visual hierarchy, as you can attach importance to elements and even create sub-sections that can lead to further work.

1.14
Research + Practice
Planning Unit

This poster for a lecture on research and practice uses the <u>metaphor</u> of an iceberg. The clean, polished tip of the iceberg (representing practice) hides the chaos and activity below (representing research).

Metaphor
Metaphor is a means of creating a comparison between two different things. Closely related to an analogy, it transfers the meaning of one subject or object, and applies it to another.

Research + Practice
A Typographic Research Initiative/ University of Salford event

T. planning unit

In Practice...

How important is research in practice? Do designers still use sketchbooks? Is there enough time to work on projects that are not profit driven?

These issues will be debated by key members of the design community and academic staff from the school of art and design in this symposium.

Date: 29/02/12
Location: University of Salford Media City Building. Room 2.36. 2-4pm.

Entry is free, please contact Sophie Williamson to confirm your attendance s.williamson@salford.ac.uk

Keynote Speakers
Nick Hard + Jeff Knowles
Planning Unit

Planning Unit will be joined afterwards for a panel discussion, Q+A on the topic of research and practice by:

Mark Janson
Creative Managing Director
Eskimo Creative

Paul Heys
Educator + Graphic Designer,
University of Huddersfield

John Rooney + Tim Isherwood
University of Salford,
School of Art and Design

1.14

Idea generation does not need to be a solitary activity; in fact, it is often easier to come up with innovative concepts when you have other people to bounce thoughts off.

The techniques covered through the first section of this chapter can be taken on as a group or alone, but the next few pages look at techniques that give the best results if taken on with other people.

Visioning

Visioning is a group activity that aims to ensure that group work has a clear direction and goal. It can be a valuable way to start your collaboration, as defining a shared goal is often the greatest stumbling block for team-based activities.

When starting a session, appoint a facilitator and a note taker. The facilitator should make sure that the activity moves forward in a positive way, and that everyone in the group has input. The note taker should record the dialogue; this is best done on a flip chart if you have access to one, so that the group will be able to refer back to it easily.

Firstly, the group should talk about what they are trying to achieve – discuss the brief and thoroughly define the design problem. All members should talk about their current knowledge of the subject, and identify what they need to learn (as well as the tools necessary to help them do this).

The best visioning sessions are fast-paced, but they should always be forward-thinking. You should try to forget barriers that may stand in your way, as these can constrict the quality and volume of the ideas produced.

Normally one focus of visioning activities is looking ahead and considering where technology and culture is going; this is a good starting point as it will get the group thinking about the context the final designs will exist in. From here you can start to think about what can currently be achieved and practical ways of moving the project forwards.

1.15

1.15—1.17

Twenty-Five Gold Facts
re-shape invent

Twenty Five Gold Facts was produced for the 25th Goldsmiths' Livery Fair, to showcase the extraordinary history, qualities and potential of gold. Detailed tests were conducted to ensure the foil-blocked cover used just the right weight to achieve perfect results. This is a simple idea, perfectly executed.

1.16

EPI/Marsden
1Kg
J7463 O/S Pantone® Gold 872
Precision House Ring Road Seacroft Leeds LS14 1NH

Provocation (shaking it up)

When a problem appears to be unsolvable you may find yourself making extreme or flippant statements about it; provocation is a way of working that attempts to embrace this. It is a method that opens up the group to far-fetched suggestions, and then attempts to rationalize them.

Provocation is sometimes referred to as 'po'. This is one of many lateral-thinking exercises developed by Edward de Bono. Introducing unexpected elements into your thinking can disrupt your normal patterns of thought development, which can often lead to new, innovative ideas.

If, for instance, you are struggling to make a product stand out in a crowded marketplace, you could pose questions that seemingly oppose the brief. You might take the reverse stance and ask, 'How can we better hide our product?'. Or you could exaggerate possible solutions by stating, 'Make it bigger and bolder'. You can also distort the thought process by adding humour and ludicrous elements. You could create a wish list of solutions that currently seem impossible, by asking questions like, 'How do we make this the only product a consumer would consider?'.

These questions can all be answered with similarly far-fetched answers, but eventually you will find threads that lead to viable resolutions. The value of po is to allow intermediate, obscure, or even silly ideas to form in order to allow subsequent ideas to follow.

If you wait for opportunities to occur, you will be one of the crowd.

Edward de Bono

Edward de Bono
De Bono is a widely respected proponent of approaches to thinking. His methods, including lateral thinking, have been adopted around the world. Many of his techniques are based on the idea that creativity is something that can be learned, rather than being instinctual. 'One very important aspect of motivation is the willingness to stop and to look at things that no one else has bothered to look at. This simple process of focusing on things that are normally taken for granted is a powerful source of creativity,' explains de Bono.

1.18
EUCLID
Reform Creative

Standing out in a crowded marketplace often involves changing perspectives, style and even scale. Creative director Paul Heaton explains the thought process behind this example: 'This print piece was produced to promote a website that offered arts and culture videos. The idea was to create an oversized, retro cinema ticket. The ticket was printed in two colours at A4 (8.2" x 11.7") size on an uncoated, authentic stock and then die-cut to shape. We produced 20,000 and distributed them to a wide audience which increased website visits by 50 per cent.'

1.18

Rephrase the question

In some instances research and idea generation go hand in hand. A brief can often be broken down into a series of questions that need answering – all of these will need to be answered with good research, and then responded to with your ideas and concepts. Asking the right questions will help to focus this process and make it go smoothly.

Firstly you should consider exactly what you are being asked to investigate, and then determine what actions you may need to undertake to get you to your goal.

With the statement, 'we want to be the market leader', it could be argued that the client is asking, 'why do we sell less than other brands?'. However, this could be rephrased positively with the question, 'what can we learn from our competitors?'. Consider whether you are looking at a graphic problem, or perhaps one of perception.

You will find that a brief often needs to be redefined in this way, as a client may not always know exactly what they need; you are the expert and it is your job to guide them by asking the most relevant questions. Questions demand answers, and these should be based in evidence.

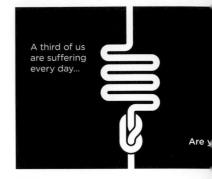

A third of us are suffering every day...

Are y

1.19

1.19—1.20
Love Your Gut
Karoshi

This campaign for the fermented milk drink Yakult is targeted at the potential millions of people suffering from digestive health problems. A simple, iconic device is used to distil the message into a simple, memorable form.

Asking a simple question is often the best way to engage with your potential audience, and this campaign is intentionally accessible through the use of bright colour and clear symbolism.

Tip #5 – Ask questions

- If you are stuggling to reach an answer, ask questions. What are the limits? How could this be different? Why am I assuming it has to be a certain way?

- If you are still struggling, rethink the question. Albert Einstein famously said, 'problems cannot be solved by the same level of thinking that created them' – in essence, turn it on its head.

Random word (association)

If you hit a dead end with idea generation processes, throwing something unexpected into the mix can really help. By attempting to bring ideas together that are not connected you will instantly shift the way you are looking at things.

Random input can come in the form of a word chosen from the dictionary, or an online random word generator. Once you have a word, consider how it could be coupled with your project – think about what it may suggest, and see what associations it brings to mind.

Nouns will make you think about how you can connect two things; if your brief was to undertake a branding project for a restaurant, and the random word was 'school', this could suggest any number of things – blackboards, lessons, writing, and so on. A verb such as 'run' or 'fall' might suggest how a concept could work, as they suggest movement and action. An adjective such as 'big' or 'round' will make you think more about how you could describe your designs, and this can be from a positive or negative point of view – this will help you consider what you do, and do not, want to achieve.

The combination of your initial ideas and the random word provides a starting point that can lead to innovative concepts and solutions.

1.21—1.24
Over the Moon packaging
The Creative Method

This packaging was created for the Over the Moon dairy company in New Zealand. Creative director Tony Ibbotson worked with typographer and illustrator Andi Yanto to create the imaginative, text-based packs. As a newcomer to the marketplace, Over the Moon needed to stand out immediately, to compete with established rival brands.

The packaging takes a contemporary hand-crafted approach, based on the 'Hey Diddle Diddle' nursery rhyme. Rough, white type is used on a black background, creating the look of a blackboard. The use of words creates an engaging and approachable graphic with a hint of humour.

Tip #6 – Random word

- Immediate thoughts are often the best.

- Don't look for immediate associations with your project – explore.

- Try multiple words, as you will grow a bigger picture.

- Work with every word chosen, no matter how odd!

1.21

the cow jumped over the moon, sounds like bull !

COTSWOLD
Product of New Zealand

Qty : 2.856 kg
ce : $11.25

over the
moon

:25:42

1.23

1.24

The packaging takes on a blackboard feel
to link with the delicatessens where the
products are sold.

Tony Ibbotson, The Creative Method

Studio interview:

Hat-trick Design

Hat-trick Design are a multi-award winning UK-based creative agency. They work for a wide range of clients including The Royal Mail, The Natural History Museum and Action on Hearing Loss. Their work, be it identity, film or print, has a signature of creativity and imagination that is both informative and playful.

Are there any processes you have developed to help kick-start the idea generation process?

Thinking about things a lot. Working all the time on trains, in pubs, in the bath, when walking about…You need to get lots of references, keep feeding your brain with film, art, music and discussion.

We often sit down around a table to discuss a project with very little to go on, and then get up an hour later with loads of possible ideas.

How do your best ideas occur?

When you least expect them.

Often for me it's when I'm sitting on a train and the beginning of an idea forms. It's when you share and discuss that idea that it becomes more fully formed and much better.

When do you know you have the 'golden idea'?

I always find it difficult to know when I've thought of anything good. I get very excited about ideas, like a child, but I do that about bad ideas as well!

The key moment is when you show it to someone else and you really want them to like it. If they don't get it, you want to convince them – that's when you know in your heart it's a good idea.

What are the most effective ways to communicate your ideas?

If the idea is good, you can usually tell someone about it without any visuals.

Do you ever have creative blocks, and if so, how do you overcome them?

Often. Just keep working away. Ideas are there to be discovered.

The best ideas seem to occur just when you feel really stuck and cannot see a way forward. Then you think of something, and it seems like you should have thought of it all along.

Shown are a set of stamps celebrating the 350th anniversary of The Royal Society. The brief was to showcase the achievements of the society, and communicate how the work of its fellows, past and present, has had a remarkable impact on the world. The Royal Society is the world's oldest scientific academy in continuous existence and the stamps chart some of its rich and prestigious history.

The split design of the stamps meant we could pair the luminaries' portraits with dramatic, colourful, brainstorming imagery, representing their achievements.

Jim Sutherland, Hat-trick Design

The number of people voting in general and local elections is declining, especially within younger age groups. You will produce a mind map to explore the reasons why this may be the case. You are not asked to come up with solutions to the problem – just to explore and note any associations or thoughts that occur to you through the exercise.

Brief

Start from a central point on a large piece of paper (A3/11.7" x 16.5"), and write the word 'voting'. It is a good idea to make this first mark large and bright, as it will become the focus of the activity.

From this point you should create a second tier of associations, positive and negative – these will form the basis of your exploration. Next, take each word in this second tier and find as many associations as you can, but don't worry about these terms linking back to the original concept.

Repeat this step until you have filled the page and then step back and consider whether there are recurring terms and themes. Are there any obvious links between different strands and layers? Is there anything that really stands out?

Any of these 'stand-out' terms can then be used to help you think about the original problem in a new way, and explore the issues with fresh eyes.

Project objectives

- To gain a better understanding of the use of mind mapping and realize how it can apply to any context.

Recommended reading related to this project

de Bono, E (2007). *How to Have Creative Ideas: 62 Exercises to Develop the Mind*. Vermilion

de Bono, E (1990). *Lateral Thinking: A Textbook of Creativity*. Penguin

Ingledew, J (2011). *The A–Z of Visual Ideas: How to Solve any Creative Brief*. Laurence King

Lupton, E (2011). *Graphic Design Thinking: Beyond Brainstorming (Design Briefs)*. Princeton Architectural Press

Chapter 2 – Creative thinking

This chapter provides key strategies, methods and games for generating ideas, drawn from a wide range of disciplines. Applying these approaches to design practice can be a very productive way of generating a variety of innovative concepts and design solutions.

Examples from professionals, theorists and students are explored from a practical point of view; this will help you realize design outcomes that go far beyond the obvious.

There are many puzzles, prompts and games that can be used to help stimulate creative thinking and the idea generation process – this section will give an overview of some of the best recognized.

The outcomes of these activities will not necessarily be fully-fledged conclusions, but they will suggest paths and fields of study that will be worth exploring. To achieve the best results, you should use multiple approaches, then judge the results in terms of common areas and those likely to prove most useful in relation to the brief.

All of these methods are designed to get you thinking outside of your comfort zone and considering the most extreme solutions to a given brief. Some of the ideas and concepts arrived at may be strange and may not appear to bear relevance to the initial problems. These should not be discarded as the process of synthesis will help rationalize them and further work may transform them into workable and innovative solutions.

2.1

2.1—2.5
Orphan
Sam Winston

Collated scraps of paper were used to construct this artist's book. The process of collection informs the work, which is an experimental piece of research into the act of writing and letterforms.

2.2

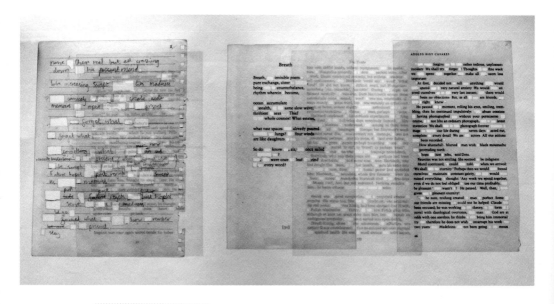

2.4

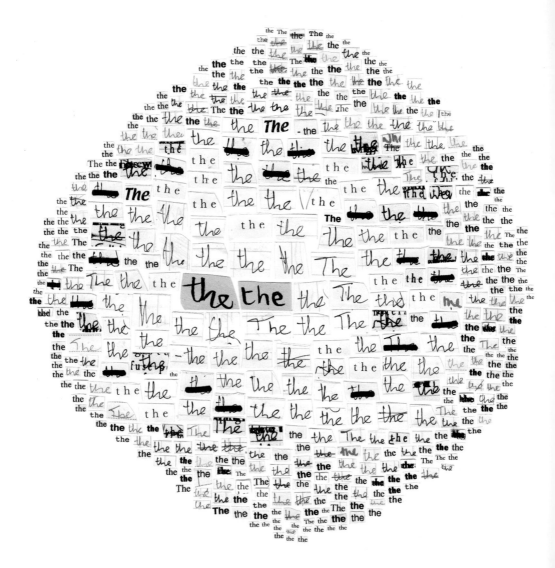

2.5

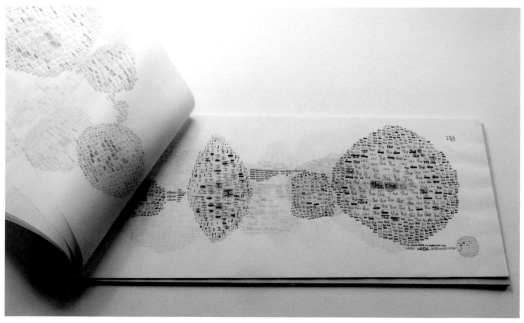

Free association

Free association can be approached by taking one element, or trigger, from your brief and then considering as many associations as possible. The elements you associate need not be connected to the project as a whole, just to the part you are concentrating on. This could be an image, colour, word or brand value.

Once you have generated around 20 associations you can start to explore each of them individually and create a new set of associated terms. You should repeat this exercise for about an hour. This can be done in the form of a mind map, or through group discussion. Conducted in a group, these activities can achieve quick and varied results that draw from a large pool of specialist knowledge.

Whichever way you choose to approach free association, you should allow yourself to go off track before beginning to refocus on the project at hand. You should give yourself enough time to really explore and forget the brief (one benefit of working in a group is you can assign strands), and then start to look at the data you have amassed.

Once you have a body of work to sort through, you can divide it into categories for evaluation. Start to look at the terms that you feel will be most advantageous to your project, then those that may be useful later, and finally the terms that you do not feel will be useful to your project at all. From here you should look at the implications of each association and consider what it might mean to the overall brief or project. This will help you create ideas spontaneously. If done quickly, it will help access your subconscious and reach surprising ideas.

2.6

Index on Censorship **magazine cover**
Andy Vella

Index on Censorship is an organization that promotes freedom of expression. This issue of their magazine focused on women who censor; represented by the arresting image of a woman's mouth. By being rotated, the image presents a duality of meanings relating to sexuality and the perception of femininity. Andy explains, 'A woman's mouth, sewn up and silenced but still wearing lipstick, created a powerful passive/aggressive visual statement.'

Tip #7 – Free association

- Try to work with others to gain a broader understanding of the subject.

- Make sure everyone in the group feels they can input.

- Choose words that stand out – they might be repeated, or look out of place in the brief.

- Always take time to refocus and reflect.

2.6

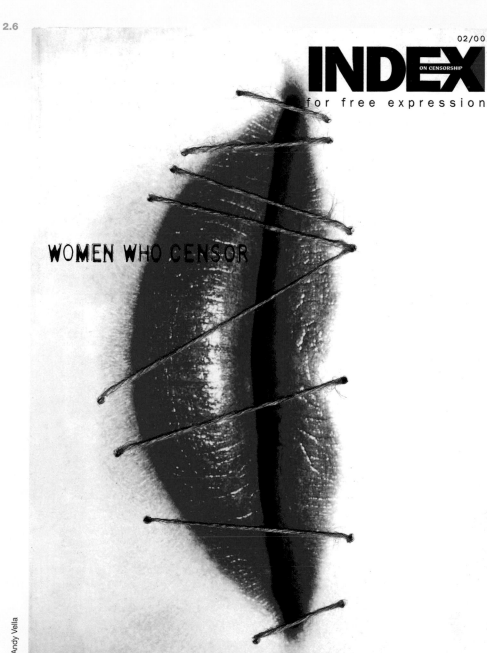

2.7—2.8
'Goth' characters
Matthieu Delahaie

These illustrations by Matthieu Delahaie are a representation of the familiar, almost ubiquitous Disney characters (Donald Duck and Mickey Mouse) presented in a subversive, 'gothic' style.

As discussed on the previous spread, free association can create ideas spontaneously, accessing your subconscious to produce surprising ideas such as this.

2.7

2.8

Word association

There are several forms of word association that can be employed to reach different goals within a project. As a game, word association can help you reach concepts quickly and examine other people's thoughts, feelings and associations with a particular concept.

It works by getting a number of people to stand in a circle and then picking one person at random to start with a word that you assign, or ask them to choose one from a list of terms that are related to the project. The person will state the word, then the person to their right will say a word that they associate with it, then the person to their right will react in a similar way to the newest word, and so on.

You should record the words as they are said. The activity should be fast-paced and you should put a time limit on it. Once you have reached the end of the game, compare the first and last words, and look for the thread that people followed – this will give you an insight into the group's thoughts on your project.

You can also approach this in a more formal and targeted way, in the manner a marketing company would. To be more precise and measured about the data you collect you can pick a single stimulus (an object, campaign or brand) and ask a number of people for a few words that they associate with it. You will quickly establish the most common words and get a good picture of an audience's perception.

Word association can also be used when working alone by referring to a thesaurus, dictionary, or one of the many online tools such as the random page function of Wikipedia.

Random

The notion of randomness is complex, as it isn't simply a lack of predictability. To be truly random, techniques and devices need to be implemented to remove the selection processes we all naturally use every day, often without even realizing it. Even when true randomness is applied, there are frequently patterns that occur. In drawing lottery numbers, for example, there are numbers that occur more often than others.

2.9
Word Bumps
Tanner Christensen

The Word Bumps website (wordbumps.com) presents a series of snippets of writing from a rich and varied pool of sources. This introduces the element of chance and randomness, exposing the viewer to subjects and writing styles they may never otherwise have considered.

Tip #8 – Read random things

Make a habit of reading things you wouldn't naturally choose. Pick a page of a dictionary, look at every tenth magazine in a store, blind-buy a box of books from a junk store – it really doesn't matter where you take inspiration from.

ᙡ WORD BUMPS

Bits of inspirational writing. Think of this as an online gallery of writing that both inspires and moves you. A collection of favorable words from writers of all different types.

For the past decade or so, the only critics of science fiction I pay any attention to, all three of them, have been slyly declaring that the Future is over.

Posted May 24th, 2012

Like many people, I like to set aside a few hours every day, generally between 3 and 6 a.m., to lie quietly thinking about everything that could go horribly wrong with my life…

Posted May 7th, 2012

He had been invited to the great feast of marriage and the banquet was rudely snatched away from him before he had done more than sample the hors d'oeuvres.

Posted May 5th, 2012

Older »

ᙡ WORD BUMPS

Bits of inspirational writing. Think of this as an online gallery of writing that both inspires and moves you. A collection of favorable words from writers of all different types.

I spend a lot of time in solitude, and a lot of time in nature. I also go swimming every day. When you go to the woods, or to the desert, or to water, and you consider your ideas, if the ideas seem timeless and valid in places like that, then they are probably very good ideas.

Posted May 1st, 2012

I remember them. They exist in my mind — in countless minds. But in a century the human race will have forgotten them, and me as well. Nobody will be able to say how we sounded when we spoke. If they tell our old jokes, they won't know whose they were.

Posted April 13th, 2012

Deep in the pages of the 28th self-help book you bought, lies the perfect piece of wisdom. It's simple and brilliant, and best of all, only $12.95.

Posted April 4th, 2012

« Newer

Older »

Lateral thinking

'Lateral thinking' is a term coined by Edward de Bono (see page 30) that describes a way of working around a problem in a fashion that rejects the normal routes. This is sometimes referred to as 'thinking outside of the box' and is used to stimulate thought in many different disciplines.

When you are faced with a design problem and there seems no obvious way of solving it, lateral thinking can be a good way forwards. The term covers many techniques that will help you look at an issue from different points of view and challenge your preconceptions; these will offer alternatives to the sequential approach many take when faced with a problem. They will often lead you to unexpected places and are a good way to get idea generation moving forwards.

By simply asking why something is the accepted way of doing things you will begin to question the logic behind it. To extend this further you can look at the rules associated with your discipline and create arguments that you feel could disprove them; this will either prove the established rules are correct and should be adhered to, or help you consider better, more innovative or radical options.

Tip #9 – Stop seeing obstacles

Turn obstacles into opportunities.

'The biggest secret of truly productive creative people is that they embrace obstacles, they don't run from them. In their mind, every setback is an opportunity, every limitation is a chance. Where others see a wall, they see a doorway.'

Ernie Schenck – *The Houdini Solution* (2006)

Divergent and tangential thinking

The word 'tangent' is often used to describe things that go off-topic, but it also suggests things that are connected at a certain point. Tangential thinking allows you to think freely and flow from one topic to the next, following any loose connections that come to mind. It encourages you to seek connections between the elements you pick, and consider why you are making particular associations. This information will help you better understand your relationship to the brief, and through this think about how the audience may be similarly affected.

Divergent thinking is the process of considering as many options as possible – these may arise from tangential thinking, lateral thinking or mind mapping, but often begin as a free-flowing exercise that takes place over a short period of time. One example would be to create as many logos for a fast food chain as you can in one hour, to push the boundaries of your creativity.

Each of these methods must be followed by a period of convergent thinking – a linear method of arriving at a solution that looks at the rational practicalities and refers more closely to the brief. However, the final 'rational' answer will still go far beyond that which you would otherwise have thought possible.

The secret of all effective originality in advertising is not the creation of new and tricky words and pictures, but one of putting familiar words and pictures into new relationships.

Leo Burnett

2.10

2.10—2.11
Göteborgstryckeriet
Happy F&B

Shown is a book for cutting-edge Swedish printer Göteborgstryckeriet. The printer had recently invested in new foiling and embossing machinery and this fictitious lost and found book is the vehicle for highlighting the accuracy of the new processes. Ordinary objects such as keys, badges and plectrums are given magical status in this trompe l'œil (see page 70) publication.

This design cleverly foregoes the clichés often associated with foiling (for example, car badges) and creates an object of subtle beauty. Tiny objects become extraordinary.

Radical thinking

Radical thinking encourages you to consider and voice the most extreme solutions to a problem, regardless of their feasibility or any potential problems. These solutions may not lead to concrete ideas, but will help examine exactly what the problem is by defining in the broadest (and most uninhibited) terms what the solutions are.

Firstly, a radical thinker will reject their ingrained thoughts regarding a project and attempt to get to the core of the brief by examining what the subject is and what they want it to be. This is harder than it sounds, as there is often a long and established history for why and how things work.

For example, if you wanted to sell a new brand of mobile phone, you would instantly question what the market needs and what sells in terms of shapes, colours and interface. However, a more fundamental question may be, 'Why do we feel the need to communicate and use the telephone?'. We may question how it is used, where this usage takes place and then look at the different ways it is regarded by a range of people. Once you get to the core of why people feel the need to buy a phone, and what it means to them, you can design a campaign much more effectively. With a campaign of this type the real question will not be how do we sell more products, but why do people need them?

2.12—2.13
Colour Match
Dowling Duncan

Shown is a radical rethinking of CD packaging for artist Simon Patterson's Colour Match screensaver which was sold in the Tate Modern, London. Featuring a recording of football commentator John Cavanagh reading results, the foam ball and net playfully references the subject matter. The packaging protects the artwork and acts as a point of display, but it also encourages interaction.

Tip #10 – Think inside the box

We often use the phrase 'thinking outside the box', but actually limitations can provide a positive influence on the creative process. Setting some self-imposed limitations can help to focus the mind and to generate ideas within the constraints of a given brief.

2.13

2.14

Issues with rice bags

Placement
Bulky, heavy rice bags have to be stored in low cupboards, making access more difficult.

Stacking
Stacking heavy, formless rice bags is difficult and unsafe – stacks can easily fall over.

Resealing
Loose resealing allows moisture into the bag, making the rice deteriorate more quickly and creating an environment for insects to inhabit.

Transporting
Carrying 15lb/7kg bags is a two-person job and can involve dragging the bag, causing damage to it and potentially contaminating the rice.

Pouring
To get the rice out of a large sack, many people pour the heavy bag, causing possible back injuries for elders.

2.15

Ideation sketches

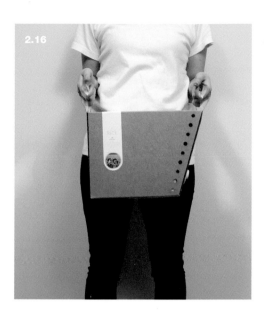

2.14—2.17
Rice packaging
Daye Kim Design

Following a series of simple steps can lead to surprisingly innovative solutions. Daye Kim identified a series of problems with traditional, bulky commercial rice packaging. Once the problems of weight, stackability, transportation, cleanliness and ease of pouring had been identified, design solutions were created. The resulting design is a clever rethinking of something we take for granted. The new packaging can easiliy be carried, stored and poured.

To help you describe your ideas and give them a solid foundation it is useful to have a good understanding of relevant graphic design terms, contexts and theories. This knowledge will also act as a springboard for your ideas as your knowledge of the subject will be more thorough.

You may also want to look at other theories and factors that have contributed to design work being made; innovation will often come about because of social and political change – graphic design does not happen in a vacuum.

Tone of voice

Designs are often described as having a tone of voice. This is created by the style, language and visual 'accent' of a design. This should be a considered and intentional choice – is a design witty, serious or characterful?

Concepts

The word 'conceptual' is often used to mean something convoluted that you have to work at. Conceptual art, for example, looks to defy viewers' expectations and present a new and challenging way of looking at the world. However, a concept does not need to be complicated – it is just another way of solving a design problem.

To effectively arrive at clear concepts you should distil or condense the information you have gathered, and consider what other factors and theories may be of use. As a concept is an idea devised to solve a design problem, you should turn the brief into a set of tasks and set parameters and objectives that will guide you through the process.

Once your concepts are firmed up you should consider ways of testing them; this can involve interviews with audience members, materials analysis and investigating the marketplace. This will not only solidify your concepts, but can also open doors to new areas of investigation. Your concepts can then be demonstrated as models, drawings or maquettes. These should be devised to clearly communicate your concepts to your client.

2.18

2.19

ONE PRODUCT STICKER
PLUS ONE TRANSPARENT LOGO STICKER = ONE COMPLETE
MILK BOTTLE

2.20

2.18—2.20
Natural Retreats (NR)
Social

This rebranding for US, UK and Ireland-based getaways provider Natural Retreats has a strong concept at its heart. Adding life, energy and wit to the tone of voice of the brand, a series of stickers are used to convey the sense of natural freshness.

Natural Retreats has a commitment to offering a bespoke service to its guests in beautiful, natural locations, and this packaging design reflects that. It has the feel of a slightly rustic delicatessen, while still feeling trustworthy and commercial.

Theory

It is valuable to inform and strengthen idea generation activities by relating your thoughts to relevant areas of design theory. This will give the ideas a base in established and shared knowledge, open new avenues of enquiry and enable you to better prove that your ideas have potential.

Chief among theories relevant for graphic designers is semiotics, which was developed by Charles Sanders Peirce and Ferdinand de Saussure, and was further developed by Roland Barthes. Semiotics can be used to describe the way that viewers take meaning from objects, images or sounds (known as signifiers). The meaning the viewer takes from an object is usually culturally specific, as understanding is based in the traditions of the location, country or context it is encountered in. For example, red in the West normally signifies love or danger, whereas in the East it signifies good luck. The way this information is passed from the item to the viewer is known as signification. This is important to understand, as design will only work if the audience has the right toolkit with which to interpret it.

Charles Sanders Peirce was also well known for developing the semantic network of association, though the original idea is an ancient one. This is the way that we describe objects and associate them with others. This association is represented as a graph or flow diagram through which the objects are represented as nodes. Two or more nodes are joined together by arcs that describe their joint associations. For example, the two nodes 'cats' and 'dogs' would be joined by the arc 'pets'.

Knowledge of semiotics and semantics will help you decipher and understand the different elements encountered during the research process as well as describing and classifying the information you uncover. From here, thoughts and ideas can be communicated to the client in a thorough and coherent way and the solutions presented will have a clear narrative.

Roland Barthes

Roland Barthes (1915–1980) was a notable and influential figure in the area of semiotics. He built on the work of Ferdinand de Saussure (1857–1913), who coined the term 'signifier' to describe the way a viewer associates a word with a culturally specific meaning. Charles Sanders Peirce (1839–1914) then developed the idea of the 'index', using it to describe the measure of a link between an image and its meaning. Barthes followed this work with the idea of 'connotation' in his book *Mythologies* (1957), using it to explain how meaning is purposefully attached to an object and how a message can be constructed.

CATS

PETS

DOGS

Abstraction

The term 'abstract' is sometimes misunderstood. Some people use it to describe a theoretical perspective that is not necessarily applied. Within the world of fine art, the term is often applied to works that do not directly reference real life. Painters such as Henri Matisse and Wassily Kandinsky would use the canvas to express feelings through the use of colour, shape and line. They applied different conventions to those recognized in portraiture or landscape art, and did not necessarily present a narrative – they spoke to the viewer in a new, abstract way.

Working in an abstract way is also an option that can be employed when rational thought has been exhausted, and obvious lines of enquiry are leading nowhere. There are many easy ways of reaching new and innovative concepts (discussed throughout this book), but do not be overly wary of presenting the audience with something that seems abstract or new.

Working in an abstract way cannot be forced; Kandinsky and Matisse worked with colour for many years before they arrived at their well-known conclusions. There is only one sure way to get the best from this way of working – experiment and remove the safety net. Be open to what you find and do not be too concerned with right or wrong; just play and see what happens.

2.21

2.21—2.22
Dehors
Qian Lu (a student at Lyceé le Corbusier, France)

Dehors, meaning 'outside', looks at the personal differences of people, and questions our sense of belonging. The cardboard letterforms are used to store personal belongings, and their construction creates a strong point of difference to the built environment in which they are photographed.

Abstraction is a mental process we use when trying to discern what is essential or relevant to a problem; it does not require a belief in abstract entities.

Tom G. Palmer

Avant-garde historical methods

Throughout the history of art there have been groups and individuals that have sought to make their audience stop and think. The motivations behind this range from political to personal, but the methods used form the basis of many modern idea generation techniques.

The term avant-garde refers to pioneers – those who challenge the confines of a genre, and innovate. Many movements within the arts are referred to as being avant-garde. The avant-garde has strongest roots in nonconformist ideas and values, some of which are explored below.

The Dadaists were a politically charged, experimental group that created work around the time of the First World War. Their work was both anti-war and opposed to the standards set within the arts. It encompassed art, design, poetry, performance and literature. This meshing of disciplines and ideas is key for those seeking to innovate and develop new contexts for design to reach new audiences.

The situationists were anti-capitalists who constructed situations through which alternative life experiences could be presented. They developed many techniques that employed randomization and combining elements. They were influenced by surrealist methods of bringing two things together to create new associations and meanings.

As a way of generating images, German artist Max Ernst created rubbings in which he found random marks to draw from. Tristan Tzara created the Dada poem, through which words were chosen and combined at random to create fresh couplings. Many lyricists employ this process.

Fluxus artists added performance elements to the process of idea generation. A piece could be performed and created at the same time, such as 'Piano Activities' by Philip Corner. Instructions, that bore little resemblance to traditional notation, were left by a piano, suggesting activities, such as 'play' or 'drop objects'. These instructions allowed for interpretation of the suggestions. Similarly, Brian Eno issued random written instructions to musicians he worked with in order to keep them thinking differently.

2.23
Poster for a Dada soirée (1923)
Arithmetic Composition (1930)
Theo van Doesburg

Shown here are experiments in composition and form by the Dutch De Stijl movement. An understanding of historical visual references such as these can help to inform you work.

2.23

Another strategy, détournement, is a process whereby elements are added to signs to change their meaning. This influenced culturejamming, specifically through the work of Adbusters, who would take existing advertisements and add subversive elements to create opposing views.

The thought processes behind these approaches can easily be applied when considering, for example, an advertising campaign or company branding. They all relate directly to how we construct meaning and visual language, as well as how we employ it in such a way that the audience is confronted with something new and challenging.

2.24
Talking Rainforest
Adbusters

The Canada-based global anti-consumerist organization, Adbusters, produced this 'un-commercial' in 2009 as a counter to 'greenwashing' adverts produced by the logging industry at the time. Adbusters has a prolific history of culturejamming and provocative commentary on contemporary culture.

Courtesy of adbusters.org

2.24

Art and design

Many current and historical ideas across art and design can help you realize your concepts, or develop new ones. For example, knowing how colour and image are perceived can help you to develop culturally appropriate designs, but this understanding can go far deeper. There are games that can be played with the viewer to make them look again, and this is especially useful when you are trying to attract the attention of consumers.

Trompe l'œil is a French term that means 'to deceive the eye'. This can be achieved in many ways, but most commonly with the use of optical illusion. Perspective and depth are alluded to within a two-dimensional image. This can be especially useful as a means of confounding the expectations of the viewer and attracting their attention.

This influenced op art (also known as optical art), a movement that sought to represent motion and depth in a way that relied on pattern. Arrangements of colours and shapes were free of context and existed only to interact with one another, and the viewer.

The ideas behind this owed a lot to the teachings of the Bauhaus's Walter Gropius. Many other notable artists from the Bauhaus, such as Josef Albers and Wassily Kandinsky, studied the effects of colour and how it is perceived.

2.25
Escaping criticism
Pere Borrell del Caso

Del Caso's painting of 1874 is a classic example of a trompe l'œil. The boy emerging from the picture frame blurs the distinction between the two-dimensional and the three-dimensional – literally emerging from the picture.

2.26
Nadine Gordimer book covers
Andy Vella

This series of book covers for Nadine Gordimer, former Poet Laureate of South Africa, features imagery that creates a sense of illusion. The illusion of torn paper and trompe l'œil shadows creates a feeling of depth and interest. 'I wanted to create images that would make readers do a double-take. The book is made to look 3D using cut paper, photography and shadows to fill in the gaps and in some cases suggest the image, although they are missing,' explains designer Andy Vella.

Tip #11 – Don't wait for a spark

Don't wait for inspiration, the creative spark is ultimately going to be the result of a pragmatic, structured working process.

'Studying the Wrights' (Orville and Wilbur Wright, creators of the first aeroplane) diaries, you see that insight and execution are inextricably woven together. Over the years, as they solved problems like wing shape and wing warping, each adjustment involved a small spark of insight that led to others.'

R. Keith Sawyer – *Explaining Creativity: The Science of Human Innovation* (2012)

2.26

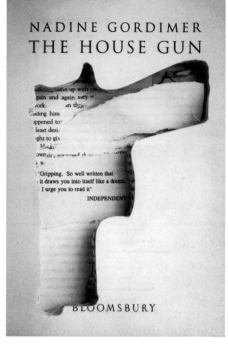

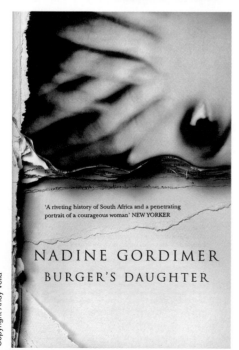

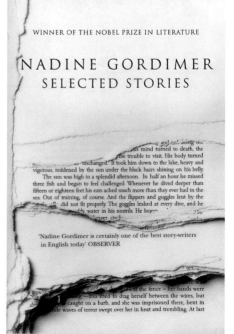

Copyright Andy Vella

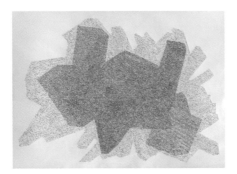 

Through his explorations of language, Sam Winston creates sculptures, drawings and books that question our understanding of words, both as carriers of messages and as information itself.

Are there any processes you have developed to help kick-start the idea generation process?

I'd say for me idea generation is a lot more evolutionary than it is 'flash of lightning'. I often watch things grow. I have a stream of thoughts, some of those thoughts are creative and if one reoccurs over a month or so I will give it more focused attention by realizing it, whether that's a drawing, design or a piece of writing. I don't know why certain themes come back more than others, but I am usually caught on language and how we use it, both visually and in terms of how it's structured. Recurrence is where a good idea comes from; if it appears three or four times, I then have to act on it.

How do your best ideas occur?

I don't keep a notebook, diary or any formal way of recording ideas. I leave enough room in the day for intuition or the unconscious to work. I meditate in the morning, as that's a more direct way of looking at the mind than indirect ways, like daydreaming. I will consciously walk into the studio and *not* think about ideas – my friend has a phrase that I like which is, 'keep it breezy'. I can be a little heavy handed, so I try to put a lightness of touch into how I think about things. I will not directly say, 'this is the concept time,' I will just ignore it. By ignoring it, things will appear in their own time. I think that is good, as a mode of operation.

Because of the nature of my artwork, I can spend five or six years on a project, and by the time I have finished it I will pretty much know what is happening in the next project, and the one after that.

When do you know you have the 'golden idea'?

I think one of the most integral parts to any idea generation process is being able to listen. Rather than trying to tell people what the idea is, try presenting the concept and listen to what is being said to you. It's a balance between listening, but not doing exactly what you are told – listening in a wise way, having discriminating awareness. You don't get to a golden idea; what you get is a more evolved idea, and if you have that mentality it will protect you from preciousness.

Preciousness comes from this idea that there is something that is genius, or there is something that is great. The moment you put that pressure on yourself, you're setting yourself up for a fall because ideas are never going to reach your aspirations of what a good idea is.

Shown are texts from Shakespeare's *Romeo and Juliet*, categorized into three emotional states: passion, rage and solace. The resulting collages have no recognizable letterforms remaining.

Studio interview:

Sam Winston

What are the most effective ways to communicate your ideas?

For me the most effective way is around language, especially written language, but approaching it from a visual aspect. If I'm writing a sentence I will think about all of the ways it can be visualized, going from paper stock to typeface, to the material it's printed on, and the print process itself. Those elements are ways of fine-tuning what I want to say, but I usually start with language, as that is the predominant way we all communicate. One of the most interesting things about communication is it can't be separated from the thing that carries it.

Do you ever have creative blocks, and if so, how do you overcome them?

The answer to getting rid of creative blocks is don't have creative blocks. What I mean by this is a reframe – by having the term 'creative block', it means it exists. My reframe is I don't have blocks, I have a period in which I need to reflect, process stuff, or the movement isn't to make stuff external, but to look internal.

If I go through a period of time where I'm not doing anything original, I'll be ticking over on other things. In the creative process there are certain movements, some towards contemplation and reflection, some towards creation. I don't have creative blocks because I'd call it something else that gives me more room to play with. I'd call it research and go out and find some inspiration, or I'd go out and talk to some people – the movement is towards learning and consuming stuff, and there's the movement towards doing something with it.

Sometimes there's the need to be creative, but there's not the impetus to do so, but then the question would be, how did you find yourself in that situation in the first place? I would ask myself why am I saying yes to more work when I need to be in a different place. I would then be looking at my practice asking why am I trying to force more creativity, when I'm obviously not in a place where I should be doing that.

Shown opposite is a print from the *Dictionary Story* series, exploring the pattern of words in a concrete poetry format.

This exercise will help you to explore ways of combining image and text, interacting with a viewer and controlling the audience's reading of an image. This will also help you better understand semiotics and the ways in which it can be applied in your projects.

Brief

Take a newspaper and cut out an image and headline from each page. From this you are asked to produce a series of six collages that combine images and text that are not intended to be placed together.

As you create new pairings, consider how you can combine these cut-outs, randomly or systematically, to juxtapose visual elements and create new meaning beyond those of the original context. Once this is done, consider which are most successful aesthetically, which work most harmoniously and which oppose one another.

You may wish to photograph each pairing, then compare the six final collages to the catalogue of pictures you will have generated, as this will test the strength of the outcomes.

Project objectives

- To consider how pairings of graphic elements can create meaning that would not otherwise exist.

Recommended reading related to this project

Barnard, M (2005). *Graphic Design as Communication*. Routledge

Berger, J (2009). *Ways of Seeing*. Penguin Classics

McCandless, D (2010). *Information is Beautiful*. Collins

Millman, D (2008). *The Essential Principles of Graphic Design*. RotoVision

Wigan, M (2006). *Basics Illustration: Thinking Visually*. AVA Publishing

Chapter 3 – Audience and context

This chapter will help you to uncover the ideas that will work best for your audience, through looking at how you can gain an understanding of the people who will engage with your end product and start to identify things that would appeal to them.

We also look at different aspects of thinking and idea generation which can be achieved with knowledge of formats, contexts and functions. We explore how knowledge of your audience, the context of your work and relevant graphic design processes can act as catalysts for ideas.

Talking to your audience and listening to what they have to tell you is key to success. The customer usually knows what they want and they are often happy to tell you. Once you've identified who the audience is, there are many ways you can speak to them and really get to grips with what they want, and start to compare this with your client's objectives.

Armed with the information outlined in the following pages, you will have a strong foundation from which you can develop ideas and start to explore possible design solutions.

Understanding your audience

Understanding the people you are designing for is key to generating appropriate and innovative ideas. When you are given a new brief and you need to investigate a particular audience, you should ask three simple questions:

Who is the audience?
This sounds simple, but you can define an audience in a number of ways such as age, gender, interests and shopping patterns. Many of these distinctions will overlap, so you may find that several markers define your audience, but knowing these will really help you to focus your ideas.

What are their needs?
Work out what it is about what you are designing that either appeals to them currently, or has the potential to do so. This can be determined in a number of ways, such as with questionnaires, surveys, tests or through observation.

3.1

What could I offer them?

This is the point in the process where clever idea generation is most crucial. Thinking about what you can give an audience may seem simple, but you always need to offer more than just a product or service alone. Brands and products are lifestyle items through which a consumer can build their identity; how you sell this to your audience will be one of the biggest challenges you will face.

This is often the hardest part of idea generation – ideas can be arrived at in a number of ways, but understanding your audience and creating concepts that genuinely speak to them is a skill you have to develop.

3.1

Build Your Own Wine
The Creative Method

This seasonal self-promotional Christmas mailer from design group The Creative Method features a series of transferable stickers (based on the staff at the agency), supplied with 'naked' bottles of wine to dress. In a market where you need to stand out, this is bound to put a smile on anyone's face.

Socio-political context

Looking at the socio-political factors that will affect members of your audience can lead to unexpected concepts. The term 'socio-political' comes from sociological studies that look at the interplay and relationship between the state and society. It covers a number of factors, from the laws that govern us, to how we define ourselves culturally.

Any number of socio-political factors will affect us on a day-to-day basis, from taxation to gender and race inequalities. All of these issues will in turn affect the way services and products are accessed and used. Understanding these issues allows messages to be better placed, and also constructed in a way that genuinely speaks to the audience.

To best understand these factors, observation and research are essential. Even if you feel that you know how a certain person feels about their position in society, you can never know for sure until you interact with them.

This interaction will help you to understand the way your final design will be used and where it will be placed. This will suggest possible materials, processes and functions.

3.2
Street graffiti

This piece of street graffiti questions our perceptions of migration ('migration – it isn't a crime'), through the use of the children's programme character, Paddington the Peruvian travelling bear.

Copyright: Chris Loneragan

A few observations and much reasoning lead to error; many observations and a little reasoning to truth.

Alexis Carrel

Tip #12 – Don't dawdle, doodle

There's nothing wrong with spending time doodling – that is, letting ideas flow without consciously trying to control them. If you don't know where to start, just start and stop dawdling.

Observation

Observation is one of the best ways to understand your audience and the context you are creating ideas for, but determining what you are looking for and differentiating it from everyday visual clutter can be difficult. It is helpful to set goals and look for specific things (no matter how big or small), such as the behaviour of consumers, different colour palettes, use of typography or visual conventions.

These initial aims will help you monitor your success and find a focus. You may only need to look for one or two things, such as whether a product is noticed on a shelf, or if people understand the way to get in and around a shop.

Detailed observation can be conducted on a small or large scale, but your choices should be dictated by the brief. For example, if you are creating point-of-sale and wayfinding devices for a department store, you should watch people in that environment and observe how they interact with products, signs, displays and one another. This should help you uncover problem areas, and help you generate ideas about how things can be improved.

Monogram
A design using two or more letters, usually the initials of the name of a person or organization.

People-watching can be a real help when it comes to understanding consumer behaviour, but if you are generating ideas for a specific product it may be more relevant to watch a single person, or a small group, and interact with them. You will often find targeting individuals to be more beneficial than watching a large group of people as you can look out for small details and focus on people to quiz about their choices. This can be extremely useful, as you can ask them why they made certain choices – was it product placement, loyalty or design?

You should always be clear about how you will record your observations and how you intend to extrapolate the data. Methods include video, photographs, sketches and notes. There are far fewer formal types of observation, such as the flâneur (see page 126).

3.3

3.4

3.3

The Only Pub Company
Haime & Butler

The shape of the 'U' is an indication of the company's activities.

3.4

Christopher Grace
Haime & Butler

This bespoke jewellery designer's identity takes the form of a <u>monogram</u> of the initials C and G.

3.5

3.6

3.5

E3
Haime & Butler

This monogram for Workspace Group's E3 strategy, implies connections and a sense of inclusion.

3.6

Digital Brookdale
Haime & Butler

Digital Brookdale's monogram is constructed using the negative space of the counter of the capital D.

Interaction

The ways in which you will interact with your audience to get results is something that should be considered when starting to generate ideas. It is useful to discuss your ideas with the audience that is likely to encounter the finished product, and also to have conversations that will help you move forwards and uncover information that may lead to effective concepts.

These interactions will vary greatly depending on what you are trying to achieve; some will be based around fact-finding and involve meeting with people face to face, whereas other meetings could involve gathering feedback in a more remote way (online or video conferencing).

Informal meetings are a good way to get on the right side of the people you are trying to speak to, and are especially useful when you are trying to gauge opinion and get an overview of a subject.

When you are trying to test ideas it is a good idea to hold more formal meetings. The reason for this is that you will need to monitor what is being said in a scientific way to ensure that your results are provable and carry weight.

3.7—3.8
The New Zealand Cheese School
The Creative Method

Creating an identity often involves conveying two things at once – a two-in-one approach. In this example, a series of die-cut holes in the shape of New Zealand convey both the product and the product's provenance. Tony Ibbotson of The Creative Method explains, 'The stationery needed to be bold, simple, immediate and memorable.' All this was achieved with the delicate addition of holes!

3.7

3.8

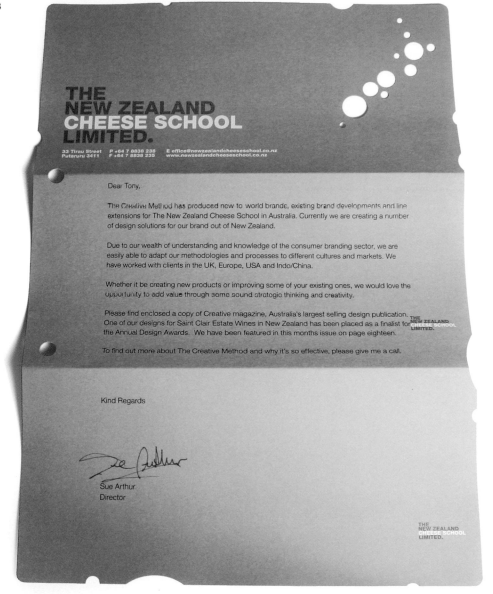

THE
NEW ZEALAND
CHEESE SCHOOL
LIMITED.

33 Tirau Street   P +64 7 8838 238   E office@newzealandcheeseschool.co.nz
Putaruru 3411   F +64 7 8838 235   www.newzealandcheeseschool.co.nz

Dear Tony,

The Creative Method has produced new to world brands, existing brand developments and line extensions for The New Zealand Cheese School in Australia. Currently we are creating a number of design solutions for our brand out of New Zealand.

Due to our wealth of understanding and knowledge of the consumer branding sector, we are easily able to adapt our methodologies and processes to different cultures and markets. We have worked with clients in the UK, Europe, USA and Indo/China.

Whether it be creating new products or improving some of your existing ones, we would love the opportunity to add value through some sound strategic thinking and creativity.

Please find enclosed a copy of Creative magazine, Australia's largest selling design publication. One of our designs for Saint Clair Estate Wines in New Zealand has been placed as a finalist for the Annual Design Awards. We have been featured in this months issue on page eighteen.

To find out more about The Creative Method and why it's so effective, please give me a call.

Kind Regards

Sue Arthur
Director

Understanding the client and area you are designing for will help you gain a deeper understanding of the context the final product or service will fit into. This knowledge can be gained from looking at the problem from a historical, social or political perspective. What is the client's background? What do they do and what are they known for? What are their values?

To define the needs of the client, research into their rivals and competitors may indicate where your project could go, or even highlight possible pitfalls. Comparing the client to their rivals will help you define them and the design problem in terms of what they are, as well as what they are not.

3.9—3.10

MAP Financial Strategies
Voice

This brochure for a company that specializes in financial planning for retirement creates a series of surprises. With paper engineering by Stuart Gluth and hand lettering by Don Hatcher, this innovative piece of communication is both subtle and engaging. An understanding of your audience is crucial and here a real sense of optimism and empowerment has been created.

3.9

catch the one that got away

3.10

This pop-up book was created to engage prospective clients and reinvigorate existing ones about the joys and endless motivations of retirement.

Anthony De Leo, Principal and Creative Director, Voice

Understanding the competition

Working towards inventive ideas and satisfying the needs of your client and the audience, while standing out from competitors, is a delicate balancing act. Once you've discussed the brief with the client and understand exactly what they want to achieve, speaking to consumers will help you understand the problem from another point of view.

An examination of the broader context you are designing for is essential, and the best place to start is with the brands or products you will be competing against. A good understanding of this context will not limit your ability to generate ideas, but will actually give you more information to work with. Looking at rivals helps you to determine what is special about the product or service your client is offering; this is often referred to as their USP (unique selling point). Once this is identified you can start to get to grips with how this may be promoted in relation to other brands in order to develop a tone of voice that is suitable and distinguishable from the competition.

There are many ways a brand speaks to its audience, from advertising to the design of the product and even its physical placement. Noting all of this information will help determine best practice and suggest possible design routes that you may choose to use as a base for your ideas, or to oppose if you feel the designs need to be unique and go against the norm.

Tip #13 – TIMTOWTDI

'There is more than one way to do it' is a saying that rightly argues that there is always another way of looking at a problem. Formal education tends to teach that there is only one correct answer, though of course this isn't the case. 'There should be one – and preferably only one – obvious way to do it,' was a counter to this argument that appeared in The Zen of Python (a set of ideals relating to the Python programming language). As is often the case with absolutes, they are both right.

Historical context

Understanding the history of the brand or company you are designing for will always positively influence any idea generation activities as it will give them a solid base. By fully exploring the context you are working in you can look at ideas and concepts that were previously employed. You should consider what worked well in the past and what can be improved upon, but also look for the key things that have given your client a personality and public face.

Some brands have such a strong identity that you cannot go against it; however, this can act as a base for ideas and a starting point. You may not be able to move away from some established elements, but these can be presented and referenced in a variety of different ways that are innovative and contemporary.

It is a good idea to look at the historical landscape surrounding your client in a broader way. An established company is likely to have a great deal of history that may not be immediately apparent. For example, some companies will have roots in particular places, or may have connections with certain people or groups. Once you have uncovered all you can, you will have a wealth of information that can inform your thinking and inspire ideas; this will ensure that you make wise and informed judgements that are appropriate to your client and brief.

3.11

3.11
Prudential Building, Buffalo
Louis Sullivan

Louis Sullivan's architecture was the manifestation of his belief that the function of a building is of primary importance and the form, or appearance, should be informed by this. Often referred to as the 'father of modernism,' his principles can be applied to all aspects of design.

A Form follows function.

Louis Sullivan

B Form follows function — that has been misunderstood. Form and function should be one, joined in a spiritual union.

Frank Lloyd Wright

3.12

HIVE&HONEY

3.13

3.12—3.14
Hive & Honey
Dowling Duncan

Shown is an identity and packaging for a fashion boutique selling women's shoes and accessories. The identity features a hexagonal 'o', referencing honeycombs. The packaging cleverly manages to be both luxurious and witty.

3.14

HIVE & H◯NEY

Knowing your subject inside out will really help you develop ideas. If you know what you can achieve with a material or process this will help you to develop ideas further. This extends to software knowledge, construction possibilities and knowing how your final product will be used.

As you learn more about the boundaries of your discipline, it will help you to ask questions about the nature of the work you are creating, and to extend the range of possibilities.

Form

An understanding of the form your final designs could take will help you to instantly consider a wide range of possibilities when you start generating ideas. The form of the object can refer to the construction, shape, appearance or material of the end result you intend to produce. This can be something physical, such as a book or leaflet, or it could be something without a physical mass, such as a website.

Knowledge of the materials available to you will help you consider things such as the size, weight and cost of your designs; these are very practical considerations, but are worth keeping in mind from an early stage to ensure your ideas do not go too far off track.

The user's needs will largely dictate the appearance as well as quality of finish; an object can indicate prestige if it has a high-quality finish – this will often make it more desirable.

The look of an object may also be rooted in history; there are many styles and shapes that are associated with periods of design such as the ornate appearance of art deco or the natural style associated with art nouveau. The Bauhaus taught us that form should follow function; this means the way an object looks should be dictated by its use and other design flourishes are unnecessary.

3.15—3.17
Swedish National Parks
Happy F&B

This visual identity and signage system for the Swedish National Parks was installed at the Hamra National Park. The signage has a playful interaction with its surroundings as designer Andreas Kittel explains, 'It interacts with the primeval forests, pristine mires and rare bugs of the parkland.' The selection of materials and placement of the signage creates an elegant and surprising result.

3.15

3.16

Photograph by Henrick Lindvall

3.18—3.19
Fresh12
Karoshi

A point of difference can be achieved through your choice of materials, stock and colours. Shown here are CD covers for music publisher, Fresh12. The design pays homage to simple screen-printed fruit packaging containers. Each CD uses a different colour pattern, creating a collectible series. The simple central shape simultaneously relates to the icon of a vinyl record, and the 'freshness' associated with the appropriated fruit packaging.

3.18

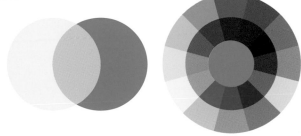

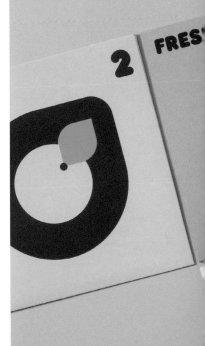

FRESH12 1

3 FRESH12 4

12 5 FRESH12 6 FRESH12

3.19

Process and function

The term 'process' generally brings to mind a very technical set of stages that will take place in a workshop. However, processes happen at every point of the design cycle, from the way you undertake research and idea generation, to the final construction of your designs.

If you are designing for print, one of the first design decisions you work towards will be the size of the final product. Knowledge of the print process will help you ensure that your ideas are achievable and cost effective. An understanding of print processes such as die-cutting will help you generate concepts and ideas that you may not otherwise have considered.

You should look to constantly update your knowledge of materials and processes as developments and updates can make construction and production cheaper, easier and more cost effective.

Understanding how your designs will be used should affect the way they are designed. For example, if the object is a handheld mobile device it may be used to access the Internet, but it will be used in a very different way to a desktop computer. The way information is viewed will be very different, as will the amount of time it is used for.

If the object is likely to be used outside, the form will have to be a lot more durable, and you will have to consider the full impact of the elements.

Other considerations you should keep in mind when generating ideas are matters of health and safety. While you do not want to limit your early thoughts, basic safety matters should be considered – such as the use of hazardous materials, or things that could cause harm. However, as with all preparatory work, limits such as these can often inspire ideas and change the way you are thinking about a subject.

Materials
Designers need to know the tools of their trade, and that goes far beyond the realms of the design studio. Knowledge of paper stocks, print processes and ink types, as well as web and media capabilities will help you to create realistic and innovative ideas and solutions.

Consumption and production

The way in which the end product is consumed will affect how it is produced. Understanding this by observing your intended audience can often inspire you to think in new ways. Once you see a product or service being used it will raise questions and thoughts as to what is currently being done well and, importantly, what could be improved upon.

The need for an audience to consume new products and services must always be weighed up against the production costs and values. Always consider whether there is a demand for your product, whether it will be profitable and, if so, whether there are sufficient production methods available to do your idea justice.

The context that the work will be seen in should affect the production decisions you make from an early stage. If your designs are aimed at an affluent and exclusive audience, then special attention will be required to ensure that the production is high quality and that the final pieces reflect this. Often this will be discussed in the brief and there will be money in the budget to cover these expenses. However, if you have a general market and the aim of your brief is to 'stack them high and sell them cheap', you should look at more affordable ways of producing the goods.

Art is the production of objects for consumption, to be used and discarded while waiting for a new world in which man will have succeeded in freeing himself of everything, even of his own consciousness.

Eugenio Montale

Studio interview:

Catherine Griffiths

Catherine is an independent designer and typographer based in Auckland, New Zealand. Her work blurs the boundaries between installation, the environment, and the commercial practice of visual communication.

Are there any processes you have developed to help kick-start the idea generation process?

Not formally. I try to remain as free in my mind as possible so that intuition kicks in, and from there I collect my thoughts, make sense, and hopefully produce a strong solution.

How do your best ideas occur?

I have no idea. I've always been open to the serendipity of life and circumstance. Those things offer more than enough to work with, whenever and however they might occur.

When do you know you have the 'golden idea'?

Have I ever had 'the golden idea'? Bronze, I recognize! If it were golden, then it might just feel *right*. Everything falls into place. It's a feeling. You just know. Perhaps the response from around you can help you realize this.

What are the most effective ways to communicate your ideas?

Using the tools that are most appropriate to express my thoughts, my ideas, my intentions. If it works in concrete, use concrete…

Do you ever have creative blocks, and if so, how do you overcome them?

As a younger designer I would fight the block. Now I just relax. I'm not so afraid. In saying that, fear can drive you places you may not otherwise go, and that can (in graphic design) be incredibly rewarding and extending. I'm prepared to take the risk. I've learned to trust my process.

Photographs by Bruce Connew

Works from *Wellington Writers Walk* (2002 and 2004) that consist of 15 large-scale, concrete text sculptures, honouring writers and poets who have strong connections with Wellington, New Zealand.

I ASK NOT ONLY THAT MY CITY, BUT ALL, GIVE THEMSELVES TO THE ESSENCE OF OUR CULT – THE RITUAL ASSEMBLY OF AN INTERESTED COTERIE IN A SPACE WHERE MAGIC CAN BE MADE AND MIRACLES OCCUR.

From Theatre in 1981: Omens and Portents

Bruce Mason
b. 1921 d.1982
CBE D Lit (Hons) Victoria University of Wellington
... include The End of the Golden Weather
... theatre critic.

Photograph by Jason Busch

Through this exercise you will experiment with using the meaning held by objects, and consider how this can be used within design.

Brief

Firstly, pick the surnames of three friends and then choose one of the following businesses:

- Sports centre

- Funeral home

- Department store

Now pick one of the following colours:

- Green

- Blue

- Red

- Silver

- Black

By combining these elements, think about the obvious graphic ideas that are suggested by each, and then how these could be combined to create a rounded outcome.

For example, if the surname chosen sounds distinguished, this may lead to you thinking of the business in the same way. If you have selected a department store and this has a distinguished name it will likely be an exclusive store. If the colour you have chosen is silver, then this may suggest futuristic reflective outcomes.

Project objectives

- To gain an understanding of how graphic elements and their various combinations can, in themselves, inspire ideas and concepts.

Recommended reading related to this project

Ambrose, G and Harris, P (2011). *The Fundamentals of Creative Design*. AVA Publishing; 2nd edition

Fletcher, P (2006). *Picturing and Poeting*. Phaidon Press Ltd

Goddard, A (2001). *The Language of Advertising: Written Texts*. Routledge

McAlhone, B and Stuart, D (1998). *A Smile in the Mind: Witty Thinking in Graphic Design*. Phaidon Press Ltd; New ed edition

Wheeler, A (2009). *Designing Brand Identity: An Essential Guide for the Whole Branding Team*. John Wiley & Sons; 3rd edition

Chapter 4 – Practical idea generation

This chapter offers practical ideas and methods that build on those described in chapter one. These will help you generate ideas both in and out of the studio.

We look at ways you can appropriate the things you see around you and build on past experiences. This is backed up by well-established theories used by many practising graphic designers and artists. Relevant theories will also be used to demonstrate how you can collect information and develop ideas in the environment, leading us to consider how we may view people in their surroundings and use this as a catalyst for inspiration.

The studio is the best environment for idea generation; when working on your own it is easy to fall back on the same tricks, or just end up feeling uninspired, but there is always inspiration to be found when you are working around others.

The studio should be a creative environment that helps you as much as any library as it should contain all the things that inspire you: books, magazines, posters, photographs, music and postcards.

4.1—4.2
Creating space to think
re-shape invent

Knowing how you work most effectively will help you create the best creative space. Usually, organization and order will help you be most productive, but some designers work with clutter and lots of material close at hand. The studio is a very personal space and you will spend a lot of time there, so make sure it feels like home.

Tip #14 – The 24-hour period

Always allow time for an idea to settle. What seems inspired late at night doesn't always seem so great in the cold light of day. Always allow time to revist ideas with a fresh pair of eyes, and always be comfortable with an idea before presenting it to a client.

4.1

Breaking apart the problem

Sometimes a problem may just seem too huge to solve. In this instance, it may help to ask yourself what you are being asked to do. What are the smaller tasks that will help you achieve this? This technique is used extensively in mathematics. For example, what is 13 x 5? It is simpler to break this into two smaller problems, what is 10 x 5, added to 3 x 5? They both arrive at the same answer, but one route is simpler and easier to follow.

Often a brief may hide, or overlook, the real design problem, so do not assume that what you are being asked to do will necessarily achieve the aim of your client. For example, a client may ask you to redesign a product because they want to increase their sales, but this may mask the problem rather than address it. Normally decreased sales indicate larger problems, such as increased competition or an issue with brand perception – these issues will need to be addressed before a change of appearance can make a real difference.

Another way of breaking apart the problem is to look at each element on its own. If you were asked to rebrand a company, you could start by unpicking their current designs and evaluating what is and is not working. From here you can address one element at a time (colour, typography, scale, etc.). You do not always need to have a big overarching concept before you start designing; sometimes smaller elements can lead to big ideas.

A design brief can also be broken apart in this way. By searching for keywords, questions and phrases, the goals will often be demystified and the true needs, wants and intentions of the client will be revealed. Before attempting to solve the larger problem presented with one grand idea, the brief can nearly always be broken down into more manageable tasks.

4.3
Bankhall
Reform Creative

This Subbuteo-inspired direct mail campaign was designed to generate leads for Bankhall (the UK's largest provider of support services to financial advisers). The materials chosen created an authentic-feeling product, with the figure tray being lined with felt. The box also contained a leaflet outlining the benefits of becoming a Bankhall member. A final humorous twist was delivered in the form of red and yellow cards, as Paul Heaton explains: 'Two weeks after the box was sent out, if a meeting had not been booked, a yellow card was sent out, followed by a red card, as an extension of the football theme.'

Direct mail
A form of marketing designed to target a pre-defined group. Direct mail has a specific, accountable aim – be it to create leads, drive sales or raise awareness.

4.3

The target audience was predominantly males in their 50s. We felt the Subbuteo figure would be well received, memorable and bring a feeling of nostalgia.

Paul Heaton, Creative Director, Reform Creative

4.4

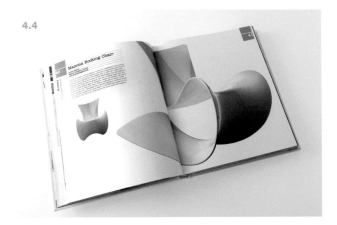

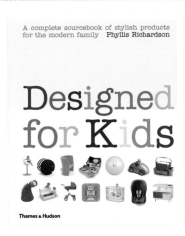

A complete sourcebook of stylish products for the modern family Phyllis Richardson

Designed
for Kids

Thames & Hudson

4.5

4.4—4.7
Designed for Kids: A Complete
Sourcebook of Stylish Products
for the Modern Family
Grade Design

These designs were produced for a resource book published by Thames & Hudson in 2008 which covers over 450 children's products. Developing an approach and a style to a design often involves immersing yourself in the content, as Peter Dawson from Grade Design explains: 'It was an interesting challenge as the content appearing in the title was obviously targeted to work for a much younger market than would actually buy the book. So reflecting a child's aesthetic in the title while still appealing to design-conscious adults was a balancing act between an innocent, primary look and one that was contemporary and authoritative.'

Light, bright and fun, the design was deliberately styled to be like a children's book in tone. The use of key lines throughout for the typography to sit on was to evoke memories of school exercise books.

Peter Dawson, Grade Design

4.6

Appropriation

Appropriation is the use of borrowed work or found objects in new pieces. There is a great history of this within popular culture and design as it is a short cut to adding value to an image. When you reference work by others that an audience is familiar with, they will bring to it a set of associations that will help them understand and engage with the work. You can begin to create new meanings and ideas by including things that do not normally go together, or by altering the context, scale or appearance of the items you are referencing – this is often described as intertextuality.

It is important to bear in mind that plagiarism can be an issue when referencing other designers' work, and work should never be simply 'lifted' as this would infringe the copyright of the original artist (even if it is only small elements of a larger piece). However, paying homage or parodying work is commonplace within most media, from *The Simpsons* to the work of Jake and Dinos Chapman.

The pop artists were experts at appropriating everyday objects, and turning them into spectacles. Andy Warhol famously used images from newspapers and enlarged them to the size of classical paintings. Through doing this, he changed the context of each item and the way the viewer perceived it – he turned the ordinary into extraordinary works of art.

4.8

4.9

> **Tip #15 – Appropriation**
>
> • Be a magpie – collect everything that stands out.
>
> • Research the copyright restrictions of any material before you use it.
>
> • Ensure that any work used is adequately transformed from its original state so that it can be deemed 'fair use'.

4.8—4.12
Casa Gusto
The Creative Method

This range of food packaging borrows from the theatrical and the nostalgic, while still being contemporary, humorous and desirable. Why shouldn't the everyday commodities we consume also delight us?

4.10

4.11

4.12

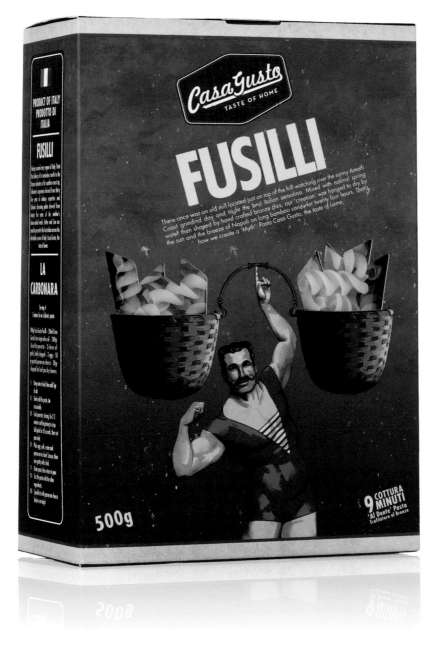

Bricolage

The term 'bricolage' comes from a French word that means 'to tinker' – it is used to describe a person who uses elements around them in a resourceful way to create new things. This can refer to objects as well as ideas. Bricolage may be improvised or deliberate, so it can be experimental or be applied specifically to a brief.

This technique is used within many postmodern artworks, from Picasso's use of newspapers in collages, to Richard Hamilton's photomontages. You can also see this applied in assemblage, which is essentially a 3D collage, made from existing objects. Russian painter and architect Vladimir Tatlin was one of the first recognized artists within this movement before others such as Man Ray and Robert Rauschenberg.

In modern times, companies have become increasingly protective of their brand identities and enforce copyright laws to protect them, making bricolage and appropriation far harder art forms to exercise. As such it is crucial to research and understand copyright issues.

You should retain any work that you create when learning new techniques, or generating new ideas. Referring to elements from previous experiments of your own, such as colours, typographic choices and arrangements, is not cheating – it is learning from what you did right and appropriating that knowledge in a new context.

4.13—4.14
The Mad Hatter's Picnic
James Kape and Briton Smith

Shown here is an invitation for an Alice in Wonderland-themed dinner and drinks event. By isolating and combining these everyday objects, something extraordinary is created.

4.13

The whole is greater than the sum of its parts.

Aristotle

Tip #16 – Follow rules / break rules

Creating a point of difference often comes from having a complete understanding of what has previously been done, and then doing something different.

'Rules are not necessarily sacred; principles are.'
– Franklin D. Roosevelt

4.14

Six thinking hats

Developed by Edward de Bono (see page 30), 'six thinking hats' is a parallel thinking process that assists focusing and the direction of your idea generation activities. It encourages you to think in six different and deliberate ways about a problem. These different ways of thinking combine to give you an overview, and a starting point for your ideas.

The six metaphorical 'hats' are attributed different colours, each signalling a different thought process. They can be applied one after another to give you a clear picture of what you are looking at, or singularly to redirect or give focus to a group meeting or conversation.

The hats represent the following attributes:

The white hat: the facts; everything you need to know about a subject.

The green hat: creativity, investigation and provocation – you will put forward creative statements and ideas to see where things go.

The red hat: think about your feelings, or your gut reaction to a subject; it is not grounded in anything that can be easily justified.

The yellow hat: positive attributes; it can be used to turn around a conversation when people are responding negatively.

The black hat: 'devil's advocate' – look for potential problems within a decision and try to identify possible flaws.

The blue hat: exert control to ensure that decisions are reached and things stay on track; this hat will be worn by the chair of the meeting.

4.15

'Six hat thinking'

Techniques such as this allow you to approach a problem from multiple perspectives. This encourages you to consider approaches you may normally discount and break away from any entrenched ways of thinking.

4.15

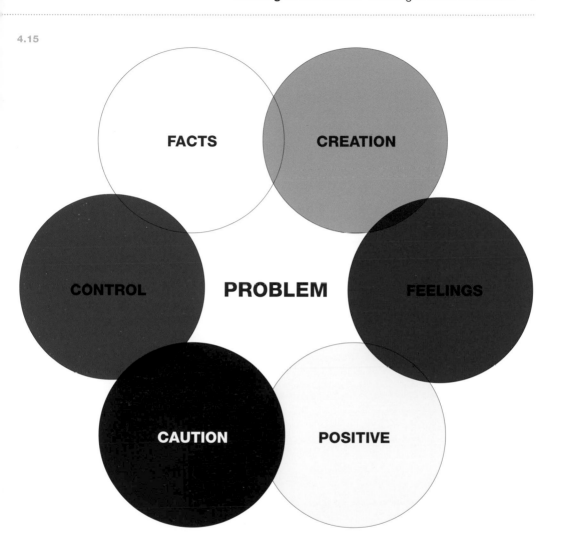

Sometimes the situation is only a problem because it is looked at in a certain way. Looked at in another way, the right course of action may be so obvious that the problem no longer exists.

Edward de Bono

SCAMPER

The American education writer and thinker Bob Eberle developed a method of idea generation that he called SCAMPER. Each of the words represented by the acronym is a verb, encouraging you to look at the design problem in different ways.

Substitute: swap things around to see what else you can come up with. This could be a change of materials, components or even context.

Combine: bring things together. You will often do this to enhance the usage or productivity of something – to make it stronger, more durable and more efficient.

Adapt: change the way things are used, or integrate it into something else. Sometimes to solve a problem you will need to change the nature of the product, service or process.

Modify: change the style, size, material or processes that are currently used. You may modify them, or you might also do this to give the appearance of newness – repackaging can be as powerful as creating something new.

Put to another use: see what else you can do with the different elements. Often when a product or service has reached its potential, you must look for a new audience or context it can be placed in.

Eliminate: remove elements from the equation. To make something more affordable, streamlined or easy to produce, look for elements that could be removed – ask yourself, what are the bare bones needed to make this work?

Reverse: using reversal when looking at a problem can be a good way to gain a new perspective – think about things the other way around, or think about ways you could achieve the opposite effect to the one desired.

4.16—4.17
BokicaBo
Nikola Arežina

Shown here are branding designs for a small fashion label. The basis of the branding was to remove, or **eliminate** all colour from the swing-tickets, carrier bags and printed items. These were also produced using recycled materials, **adapting** to market demands and trends. The website pages are constructed from a single page, which acts like a scrollable poster, **reversing** the norm for a website. **Combining** a poster format and a website creates a real point of difference for the brand.

www.bokicabo.com/en

4.16

4.17

A great way to freshen up the idea generation process is to get outside. A change of environment can bring about new ways of thinking or positive distractions. Many idea generation techniques are specifically outdoor activities, and encourage you to look at the world around you and think about the way people live.

You will begin to think about how people react to one another and manoeuvre through their environment. This knowledge will further inform how you design work for specific audiences and contexts.

Mapping and psychogeography

Defined by the situationist Guy Debord in 1955, psychogeography is a way of looking at how the physical environment affects the behaviour and emotions of the people within it. As with the concepts of flâneur (page 126), and drift (page 125), it is a way of exploring urban environments. Information is gathered simply by walking and observing life. Observations can be recorded in all manner of ways, from notes to sketches and photographs.

Mapping graphically explains the physical geography of a place. Most obviously you will look to map geographical locations, such as buildings and landmarks, by detailing the physical layout of a place and how one space relates to another. There are other things that can be mapped to explain populations, starting with their feelings about a place (a happiness index), where people congregate (footfall) and the ways they pass through it in terms of modes of transport and distances travelled (commuter studies). All of these things will help you to understand people and can be applied when you need to research particular audiences.

Psychogeography is closely related to mapping, but it concentrates more on the effect of the environment on the individual and their identity. Architecture forces people to interact with others and live their lives in certain ways; psychogeograpy seeks to understand this.

Guy Debord

Guy Debord (1931–1994) was a founding member of the political art movement Situationist International (SI) and also author of *The Society of the Spectacle* (1967) – both of which are thought to be catalysts for the Paris Uprising of 1968. Debord devised strategies such as the 'derive' to help people experience society and environments with fresh eyes. The term 'spectacle' was used by Debord to describe the way he felt real experience (or living) was being surpassed by representation through images, particularly in advertising. This implied that relationships between consumers and products were overtaking connections between people.

Drift

A 'drift' is a journey through a given environment, undertaken without a fixed idea about where you are going, being guided by your surroundings and your curiosity. The drift is often referred to as a '*dérive*', the French term also coined by Guy Debord.

You can employ systems to take you places you would not have otherwise visited; for example, you could roll dice to determine whether you take a left or right turn, or pick an object or colour, such as red doors, to follow.

The aim of the drift is to gain new experiences and make discoveries. When we make a particular journey on a daily basis, we stop looking around us and do not pay attention to the environment. When you are drifting, you will often notice much more about the people you pass and the environment you are in than you usually would, as you are relying on your basic human curiosity, and perhaps even your fight-or-flight instincts.

This is a particularly useful method of idea generation, as you will begin to think about your surroundings and how people navigate through them, interact with one another and live. You will notice things about everyday life and start to see patterns – the way homes are decorated, the cars people buy or even the way people dress. This knowledge will inform your projects, as you will better understand how people may live with your design work.

Tip #17 – Don't be too serious

Even if the project you are working on is serious, technical or complicated, it doesn't mean your approach to it must be.

'Have fun, think like a child again, open your mind to new possibilities.' – Jack Foster, *How to Get Ideas* (2003)

Flâneur

When a brief comes in, it can be useful to take some time away and observe the factors that may affect your decision-making (see Observation, page 84). The art of observation needs as much attention as your Photoshop skills – flâneur can really help sharpen the way you see.

The French term flâneur means stroll, or saunter. In this context, it describes a way of perceiving the world that was born out of the structuralist movement. Charles Baudelaire used it to describe a person walking through a city or urban environment with the sole intention of experiencing it. At the time he coined the phrase, in the 1860s, French society was undergoing major changes – working patterns were shifting as society navigated through revolution, and there was access to new forms of entertainment and fashion.

Flâneur is a means of looking at and understanding the city – in many ways it is similar to the drift (see page 125), but the observations made are discussed in sociological and psychological terms. It involves observing how the city and community works; looking at the way people act and interact with one another, what they purchase and how they dress. You then attempt to identify and catalogue social and economic changes, as well as other cultural shifts, such as social attitudes or political feeling. This recording of life and movement within the city has informed street photography, as well as areas of urban planning, architecture and psychogeography, as these all look to address the psychological impact of the environment on society.

Wayfinding is one area of design that often employs this way of thinking to help generate ideas and concepts. When walking through a town or city as part of a crowd, you can observe what guides a person from place to place – this is often much more complex than signage and can include factors such as lighting, temperature and materials. This will help you consider which mechanisms could be put in place to make the movement of a crowd more effective.

Wayfinding and signage

One of the toughest challenges for any graphic designer is creating work that sits not on the page or screen, but in the environment. Signage is the most established environment-based graphic design.

Wayfinding involves guiding people around a space, and encompasses psychology, sociology and design to create modern, urban spaces that are inviting, well organized and easy to navigate. Signage is the physical manifestation of this.

4.18

I never think of the future – it comes soon enough.

Albert Einstein

4.18

Gustave Caillebotte
Jour de pluie à Paris (1877)

Gustave Caillebotte's pictures capture the interest people started to take in their environment. Allocating time to pondering and thinking is all part of the design process.

4.19

4.20

4.19—4.22
Club Workspace
Haime & Butler

A distinctive signage system for a workspace provider reflects the flexible and approachable nature of the company. The visual language and tone of voice bring an informality and sense of humour to the system.

The branding of an environment requires detailed research. How do people use the space? What activities do they undertake there? All of these questions will help to inform the design.

4.21

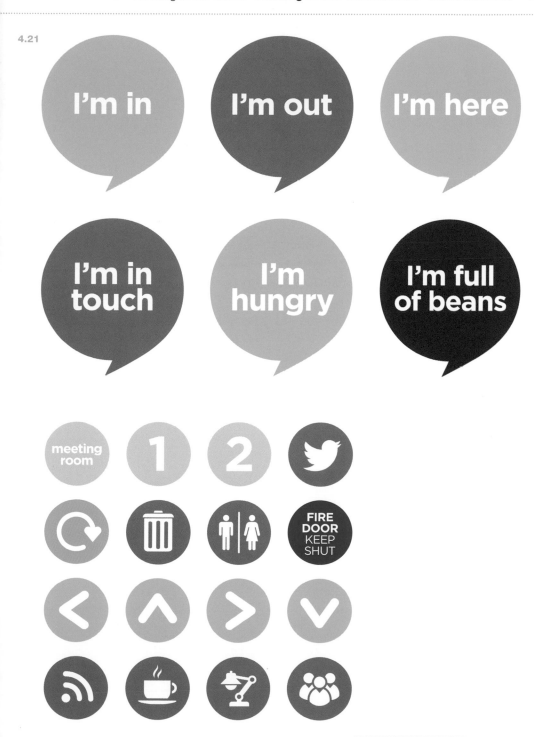

Studio interview:

James Kape

James Kape is an Australian designer currently working at Wolff Olins, New York. His work has a playful yet delicate approach to craft within a commercial context.

design stage sometimes changes have to be made pending client approval. Unfortunately this can sometimes affect a final design and the idea behind it.

Are there any processes you have developed to help kick-start the idea generation process?

I begin by referencing work and creating moods to help try to define specific directions in response to the brief. I try to find very deliberate or specific imagery to help define an idea – these images could be anything from art dating back to the 15th century to the work of other designers today.

How do your best ideas occur?

My best ideas occur when I begin to talk about them. As soon as I vocalize a thought or try to explain something, it can often grow into something bigger. I think collaboration is also key – bouncing ideas off another designer can make for a faster process.

When do you know you have the 'golden idea'?

I don't know that I have. As I create new work, I question past work and the solutions I came to. Right now, I would define a golden idea as a piece of work which ended in the result I had intended. What I mean by this is when you come to the end of the

What are the most effective ways to communicate your ideas?

Talking about your ideas and listening to how people respond – to me, this process is very much give and take. It's important to get them excited about what you're working on. Allowing their responses to have impact on what you do can play an important role in coming to a successful conclusion.

I like to talk through each of the ideas I have and my reasons for them. It's important to explain process and the intention behind what you're working on. Never assume.

Do you ever have creative blocks, and if so, how do you overcome them?

Yes definitely; good design isn't something you just do. It takes time and thought and often this can define how successful the output is. Sometimes I just need to do something different for a while, other times I need to leave my desk and go for a walk. If I put too much pressure on myself into thinking what something could be, I struggle to come to any conclusions.

Development work for a rebranding concept produced in collaboration with Briton Smith for a music festival on the Gold Coast, Australia. Eclectic elements create a playful 3-D collage. In the digital age, there is no substitute for experimentation and craft.

Activity:

Wayfinding

For this activity you are asked to consider ways that you could (safely) explore new environments. This will help you understand the elements that the general public look for to assist them with orientation and movement.

Brief

Firstly, find a place that is reasonably unfamiliar, as you want to experience this environment with fresh eyes.

Once you are in this new environment, take note of the things that you notice first. Consider the type of place you are in and describe it. Is there a 'feel' to it? Does the traffic (by car, by foot, or by other means) follow a particular flow?

To give this exercise further direction, you should record the following using a camera or pen and paper:

- Colour

- Typography

- Texture

- Advertising

Project objectives

- To better understand the factors that the public look for to navigate their way through unfamiliar places.

- To quickly grasp the elements that help people find their way.

- To understand how knowledge can be employed to ensure that people can find their way around environments you design.

Recommended reading related to this project

Ambrose, G and Aono-Billson, N (2010). *Basics Graphic Design 01: Approach and Language.* AVA Publishing

Berger, C (2005). *Wayfinding: Designing and Implementing Graphic Navigational Systems.* RotoVision

Bergström, B (2008). *Essentials of Visual Communication*. Laurence King

Gibson, D (2009). *The Wayfinding Handbook: Information Design for Public Places*. Princeton Architectural Press

Twopoints.net (2010). *Left, Right, Up, Down: New Directions in Signage and Wayfinding.* Gestalten Verlag

Chapter 5 – Developing and informing ideas

As you begin to get closer to the end of your project you will need to start rationalizing your ideas and giving them a focus that exhibits your creativity and satisfies the brief.

This chapter will help you further develop ideas and provide a path that will lead to practical outcomes. We look at how you can go about making decisions regarding the practicalities and viability of ideas and how these decisions can be tested to prove their worth.

The best ideas are those that are best informed. There are many ways you can acquire the knowledge necessary to create appropriate, viable and innovative concepts; from drawing on various sources, to exploring and dissecting the nature of the design problem and solution itself.

The tactics discussed in this chapter will help you focus on the details that make up the bigger picture. The micro to macro study looks specifically at the small details that come together to build something that really works. In addition to this, we look at ways you can identify key research sources and resources (on- and offline) that will help you understand exactly why you are looking at the wider picture, contextually and theoretically.

Micro to macro

When looking at any project, you can choose to view it as a whole (macro) or to look at the finer detail (micro). These different ways of looking at a design problem are always linked, but the route taken from one to the other can vary and will depend on the project.

Starting small and finding the design solution for each individual problem can be a better strategy than looking at the problem as a whole. For example, when looking at advertising a specific product, you may begin by talking to one or two key consumers and asking them what they want, then applying this knowledge to a concept that is presented to a larger group. Incrementally larger test groups can be assembled before the idea is launched.

Beginning with a big idea and then focusing on the smaller elements that are needed to realize it is another route. Normally a pitch will talk about the solution in broad terms, such as a line of copy, choice of imagery, placement and media type. You would then work on the details, such as layout and exact placement of elements, materials and other rendering choices.

5.1—5.2
Kotarling
Nikola Arežina

This identity for construction company Kotarling, exploits the shape of the letter 'A' in the company's name, using it to represent the roof of a house. This detail, a micro element, informs the overall design, and is realized in the folding of business cards and folders.

5.1

5.2

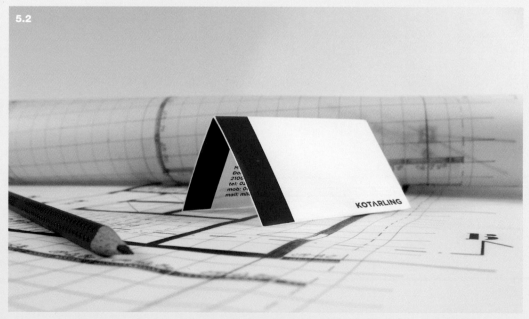

Key research and enquiries

It is vital to conduct some preliminary research to inform your ideas. Researching who you are designing for, what their requirements are and what the competition is will give you a good idea of the landscape you are looking to enter and what your designs will be competing against.

Knowledge of the audience will affect the type of ideas you generate and make sure they are on target. Understanding the ideal consumer will indicate expected usage, and the amount you can charge for your product or service – these are the parameters for your idea generation activities.

Sources and resources

There are many resources that will provide key information when you are looking to prove the viability of your ideas. Finding the right resource and reputable recourse can be difficult, as there is so much information in the public sphere regarding nearly every subject. The facts you uncover can often be hard to validate, so it is wise to look to sources that you know to be reliable and trustworthy.

Accessing key resources will very quickly make it clear that you are not the first person to have been presented with the design challenges you face. When you are finding production difficult, talking to experts, attending workshops and seminars or reading more about particular methods and skills will really help. The answer to any technical problem will be out there as there are thousands of designers throughout the world working on similar projects.

Subscribe to a few relevant email lists, blogs and magazines. Staying current is one of the most demanding challenges a busy designer faces, so accessing a few sources that you can easily engage with between jobs is a convenient way of keeping informed. In terms of more general resources, libraries are a great place to start.

Tip #18 – Inspirational blogs

There are a wide range of blogs that can serve as a valuable source of reference.

Some are shown below – but make your own list!

www.designboom.com

www.creativereview.co.uk/cr-blog

www.formfiftyfive.com

www.septemberindustry.co.uk

www.thedieline.com

www.swiss-miss.com

www.thefoxisblack.com

www.smashingmagazine.com

www.underconsideration.com/fpo

www.fubiz.net/en

www.notcot.org

www.itsnicethat.com

Using the Internet

The Internet is, of course, one of the greatest resources as it has boundless amounts of information open to anyone. It is a good place to discover other practitioners who have already uncovered solutions similar to the one you are seeking. There is also the possibility that you can contact these practitioners and ask about the choices they made.

Social networks and blogs are a great way to talk to a lot of people and get to know your audience. Networking is one of the most valuable possibilities the web offers. You can easily assemble a range of contacts through which to test concepts, and user groups that will help with the direction and progression of a project.

Be cautious of sharing complete projects with people you do not know well, however. If a concept is in its infancy, it can be hard to prove ownership of the idea – protect your intellectual property and do not share too much too early on. It is best to test fully rendered ideas (once copyright can easily be enforced) or small elements of a greater picture.

Once interesting ideas have been discovered, it is important to consider other sources that may offer supporting or contradicting ideas. Remember that any resources found online should be scrutinized carefully and their legitimacy questioned. Look for articles that corroborate the information you unearth, and try to find trusted and reputable sources that back up any dubious statements.

Curiosity about life in all of its aspects, I think, is still the secret of great creative people.

Leo Burnett

Sometimes, the sheer mass of ideas you generate can be daunting and choosing the right way forwards can be a challenge. However, there are processes that can help and chief among these is the synthesis. When there are too many ideas, synthesis will help narrow down the options until the right one is found.

From here we consider how the ideas arrived at through the process of synthesis can be further refined and developed in order to arrive at the best possible solutions, and how you may judge whether you have made the right choices in terms of your initial objectives and the discoveries made through the idea generation process.

Making choices (synthesis)

When idea generation for a project goes really well, it can be as difficult to manage as when you are struggling for ideas. Synthesis involves throwing out the ideas that are less likely to yield the required results, and narrowing the selection down until you're only left with one idea – the right one.

How to choose between the various ideas is the tough part. Firstly, you will need to redefine the parameters of the project to reflect on how the project has developed and changed – the brief you end up with is hardly ever the one you are first set.

You have to approach this process in an objective way, by removing all personal taste – look at the results with the eyes of the client and end user as these are the people who will be investing money.

Next, consider practical limitations, as some ideas are simply too costly to produce, or occasionally the processes needed to render them are not easily available. Some ideas can be scaled down, so considering ways of doing this can create more avenues of investigation.

Once you have considered these factors, the only ideas left should be innovative, practical, achievable and should suit the brief. If this is the case, the only thing left to do is choose the idea you have most confidence in.

5.3
Green Line Networks
Nikola Arežina

Designs for an Internet data mining, storage and analysis company. The various sections of the company are distinct, but connected. An overall identity is constructed from illustration style, simplified graphics and an expression of company activity through primary shapes and patterns.

Taste
Taste is notoriously hard to define, yet it is of paramount importance to a designer. You have to not only be able to refine your own sense of taste, but also be empathetic to market sectors and demographics who have their own tastes. Stephen Bayley tackles this 'notoriously elusive and nagglingly present' subject in his seminal book, *Taste: The Secret Meaning of Things* (1992).

5.3

CLOUD INSTALLATION
IN YOUR DATA CENTER

CUSTOM QUERY TYPES
DESIGNED AND AVAILABLE
UPON REQUEST

ADVANCED PLATFORM
FOR METADATA
HARVESTING

HIGH
PERFORMANCE
COMPUTING

HARDWARE AND SOFTWARE SOLUTION

Developing ideas

Once you have the idea you wish to take forwards, it is rarely the finished concept – there is always room for development and progression. A hundred different designers could render a single idea in a hundred different ways, so it is important to keep in mind that an idea and the rendering of an idea are not the same thing. If design work isn't going well, that does not always mean the concept is a bad one – it may be that you just haven't found the right voice.

Once you have an idea, the next step should be thinking of multiple ways it could work. Try testing different layouts and arrangements of shapes, consider illustration and photographic options, think about how the idea can work across media, try colour and typographic options – whatever different permutations you try, make sure you experiment and find the best possible way to represent your idea.

When looking to focus on the correct representation of an idea, you should consider what else is happening in the particular field you are designing for – are there particular material or design choices that are cropping up a lot and if so, can these be applied to your idea?

5.4—5.6
Chocodeli
Webb & Webb

Tasked with branding, packaging and designing signage for a new chocolate delicatessen, Webb & Webb developed an identity based on hundreds-and-thousands (candy sprinkles). James Webb explains, 'We wanted the pattern to have a 3D feel, so the logo is embossed – we even convinced the signmakers to build the delicatessen's fascia out of 2,500 25mm spray-painted hemispheres. Both we and the client wanted the packaging to be "fun" *and* "luxurious" – so the production values are high. We realized we had achieved this when we saw people on public transport reusing the carrier bags.'

5.4

5.5

5.6

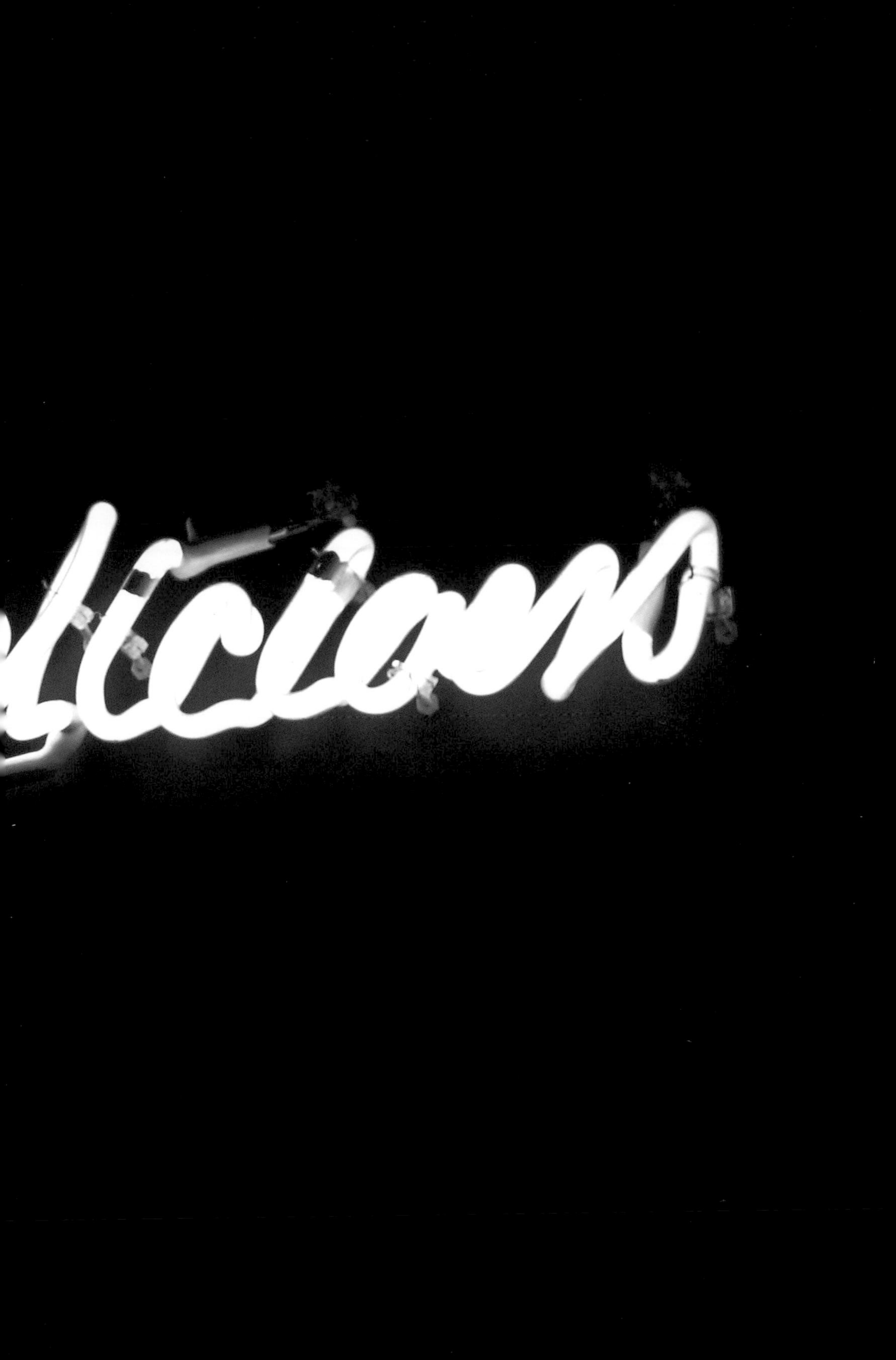
licious

Refining ideas

If you have tested and trialled an idea and you feel it isn't working, it can often be refined and developed. It is good practice not to completely abandon an idea, because of the time, research and energy you have invested in it. It is better to strip the idea back to its core elements and look for exactly what is not working. Ensure that it is the idea itself and not the rendering or presentation – when you present work to a client it is hard for them to differentiate between the concepts and the designs, so it is useful to work with them and break apart these elements. Often the design work will be a minor fix, whereas creating new concepts will mean going back to the drawing board.

To refine an idea you can test different versions on clients and user groups, or you can repeat the idea generation activities and games that led you to it. This will allow you to see if there is anything you have missed or that you could improve upon.

Observation is often key when looking to sharpen your concepts. This can be done in a number of ways, including looking at how people react to and use the product or services you are designing for. For example, if you are designing signage for a shop, the colour choices may look great in your studio, but may need adjusting once the designs are put in the context of the shop.

A broad overview of the subject and context you are designing for will also help with the final refinements; knowing how others have achieved similar feats can suggest alterations and areas that could be developed. You can then start to structure a checklist of elements that need to be refined or adjusted before the product or service is launched.

Lastly, referring back to the brief will be the final indicator of what needs perfecting; simply ask, 'Have all of the initial objectives been fulfilled?'.

5.7
Felix Hagan
Salad Creative

Felix Hagan, a composer, musician and performer, commissioned Salad Creative to design a brand that was flexible enough to be used across the different genres of his work. The resulting logo was sketched out before being rendered, and acts as a monogram.

Tip #19 – Plan by sketching

Always start a project with a sketch, as this is the quickest and easiest way to get a lot of ideas onto the page quickly. Your thoughts, eyes and hands are closely linked and sketching is the best way to quickly make visual notes without concentrating too intently on what you are doing – freeing up more brain power for creativity.

5.7

5.8

Colour

Bodoni

AaBbCc 0123 #!?

abcdefghijklmnopqrstuvwxyz
ABCDEFGHIJKLMNOPQRSTUVWXYZ
0123456789()?!@£$%&

5.8—5.9
Felix Hagan
Salad Creative

The basic design, colour and
typography were combined with
illustrative elements by Sam Alder
of moving image production
company Plastic Zoo to create
the final packaging design.

A simple yet intelligent monogram that utilizes the 'X'
of the musician and composer Felix Hagan's name.
The challenge was to allow the character of his music
or performance to sit comfortably under his brand,
while creating a distinctive and memorable identity.

Andy Russell, Salad Creative

5.9

Studio interview:

re-shape invent

Re-shape invent is an ideas-led graphic design consultancy based in London, UK. They have built a strong reputation for a deliberate and crafted aesthetic supported by the implementation of long term brand strategies, resulting in relevant and successful solutions.

Are there any processes you have developed to help kick-start the idea generation process?

At the start of each project, mood boards are produced for different themes and ideas to help identify a path of potential routes. A number of our glass walls will be covered with related inspiration, and a discussion with designers is initiated, with the possibility of client input even at this early stage. We leave the inspiration and ideas up on the walls for some time and, with the test of time and with discussion, a decision is made on where to go next.

How do your best ideas occur?

Usually a well written brief and clear understanding from the client initiates the thought process well. Ideas in general are formed intuitively and feel right and fit for purpose. It's how these good ideas are executed that is of great importance.

When do you know you have the 'golden idea'?

There is always a warm feeling and a sense that there is something special emerging. Usually there are smiling faces all around with those involved.

What are the most effective ways to communicate your ideas?

A verbal explanation always commences the communication of ideas. At this early stage this leads onto showing visuals and mood boards. We usually find that a good idea doesn't have to be shown finished and polished to be met with approval, and to progress into the development phase.

Do you ever have creative blocks, and if so, how do you overcome them?

It is always good to confer with colleagues about a project and get feedback. Bouncing ideas off one another is good practice. It's also good to move yourself into a different environment and not put too much stress on yourself. I find that the best ideas form when you are relaxed, and they are often captured while doing very different everyday exercises.

Don't view your work solely on the computer. Print it out full size, stand back and look at it with the hustle and bustle of everyday life all around. You'll notice a lot more this way about the overall presentation, not just the fine detail you see on screen.

Idea generation activities are often dependent on making links between unconnected disciplines in order to approach projects with an original viewpoint. Each discipline has its own unique way of doing things. A combination of approaches from different genres can arm you with more effective ways of achieving design goals.

Brief

Lack of awareness of other disciplines is often an obstacle for designers. To help you overcome this, you are asked to look for links between various designers, operating in very different fields.

Firstly choose two disciplines from the list below:

- Graphic design
- Fashion
- Sociology

Now pick a practitioner from each field. It is not important which practitioner you choose, but the better known they are, the more likely you will find information about them.

Research the two people you have selected and see if you can find any links between them. You should be able to find strong links by researching their colleagues, influencers and protégés – people can usually be connected through less than six linking persons.

Project objectives

- To gain a better understanding of how ideas are interconnected and can be grounded and expanded upon by researching other disciplines.

Recommended reading related to this project

Crow, D (2010). *Visible Signs: An Introduction to Semiotics in the Visual Arts.* AVA Publishing; 2nd edition

Fletcher, A (2001). *The Art of Looking Sideways.* Phaidon Press Ltd

Leonard, N and Ambrose G (2012). *Basics Graphic Design 02: Design Research: Investigation for Successful Creative Solutions.* AVA Publishing

Lupton, E and Cole Phillips, J (2008). *Graphic Design: The New Basics.* Princeton Architectural Press

Chapter 6 – Application

This final chapter will help to contextualize some of the approaches and methods outlined in previous sections and will focus on applying ideas to satisfy the design brief.

We will also explore the broader context of the final ideas and the practicalities of how to communicate and realize these by utilizing design solutions, covering a variety of platforms and contexts.

When the idea generation process is complete and there is an agreed way forwards, where should the design process go next? Presenting your ideas in a way that your clients will understand, and more importantly buy into, can be a challenge. Often the key to this is simplicity; a simple drawing may be as effective as a grand presentation if you cover the right points and are clear about what you are saying.

6.1

Communicating ideas

Having good ideas is only half the struggle – it is vital that they can be communicated in a manner that can be easily understood and appreciated by others. Ideas can be presented in a variety of ways, depending on the type of brief and the people you are communicating with.

Ideas should be presented to a client in a way that gets the key information across simply. There are short cuts that can be taken to ensure that the information is presented in a relatable way. Showing the design alongside rival brands and competitors will demonstrate its context. Presenting elements that show the wider profile of the intended audience, such as purchasing habits and brand loyalty, can help demonstrate the viability of an idea and the need for a particular approach. This will help the client understand the basis of your idea.

There are people other than the client that you will need to communicate your ideas to, so you should consider how best to reach each of them, adapting the language you use accordingly. Research groups, for example, will need some understanding of your product or service before they evaluate it, but the client will need a far greater overview, as they are the ones who are taking the greatest risk financially and with their reputation. In short – the client understandably needs the most convincing.

6.1—6.3
Garage Book
Hat-trick Design

This self-initiated, promotional book celebrates the ordinary and mundane and turns them into something magical. 'Based on observations in my Dad's garage, we wanted to produce a book that celebrated the amazing collection of ironmongery in dusty drawers and cabinets,' explains Jim Sutherland. The resulting book shows what can be achieved when you 'see' the magic of the ephemera that surrounds us all.

6.2

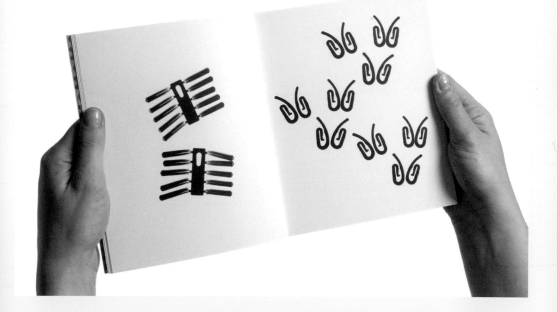

We wanted people to see more magic in the everyday...

...we wanted to turn the mundane
into a magical world full of spiders,
robots and rockets.

Jim Sutherland, Hat-trick Design

Presenting ideas

A good presentation will help all parties visualize the end product and identify areas that may need further consideration. Preparation is vital to a successful presentation. If you can confidently present your idea and justify your thought processes, the client will be far more likely to accept it as the way forwards. It is a good idea to present only what is absolutely necessary to get your point across, as anything else can be distracting.

Models and maquettes can be used to help demonstrate the size and proportions of objects being designed, as well as ideas for the materials and construction. Prototypes will highlight any areas that need to be addressed through the construction process.

6.5

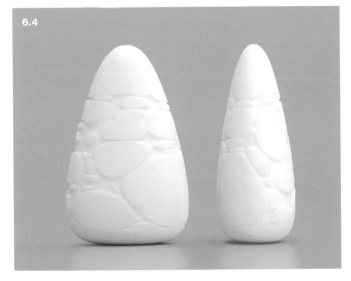

6.4

6.4—6.6

Silver Spring
re-shape invent

Shown is a re-design of packaging for the Perfectly Clear flavoured water range. Distinctive bottle shapes and label designs were explored, with the aim of raising the brand's strength across its range of products. Physical designs for three different bottle sizes were produced in collaboration with product designers, The Division. 3-D renderings were also produced in collaboration with Drive Design. Allowing the client to explore a new design in both two- and three-dimensions in this way gives additional insight and information, aiding their decision making process.

Tip #20 – Know your stuff

Working with a client often means you need to help them understand that you are an expert and they can trust you; being knowledgeable about your subject will help you achieve this.

6.6

Digital technologies can be used to present your ideas in a professional and concise manner. There are many applications that will allow you to make digital presentations that can be projected easily. Many allow you to use film, sound and other multimedia elements. It is easy to make presentations look amateurish by over-using these elements, however, so keep the presentation clear and avoid sliding and dissolving text, and transition effects.

Recent technological developments have made it possible to use <u>augmented</u> <u>reality</u> applications to create entire virtual environments in which you can display prototypes. Virtual objects can be placed into constructed or real environments and viewed using tablets or smartphones. These mobile devices allow the user to 'walk around' the object and get a feel for how it will integrate into any given context.

Augmented reality
Augmented reality (AR) presents a view of the real world *augmented* by sound, graphics, moving images or data, such as GPS information.

6.7—6.9

TEDx Portland 2012
Second Story

At the Portland TEDx after-party guests could interact with a floor-to-ceiling sculpture that transformed body movement into new physical landscapes. The theme of the conference, 'uncharted territory,' was visualized through forms and kinetic shapes that move along the panorama of the sculpture.

6.7

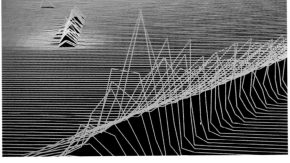

6.8

Physical reality can be abstracted and mirrored in real time to create unique experiences – in *Uncharted Territory* (shown), depth-sensing cameras create a real-time visualization, abstracting human forms into topographic contours which then stream along a sculptural form.

Daniel Meyers, Second Story

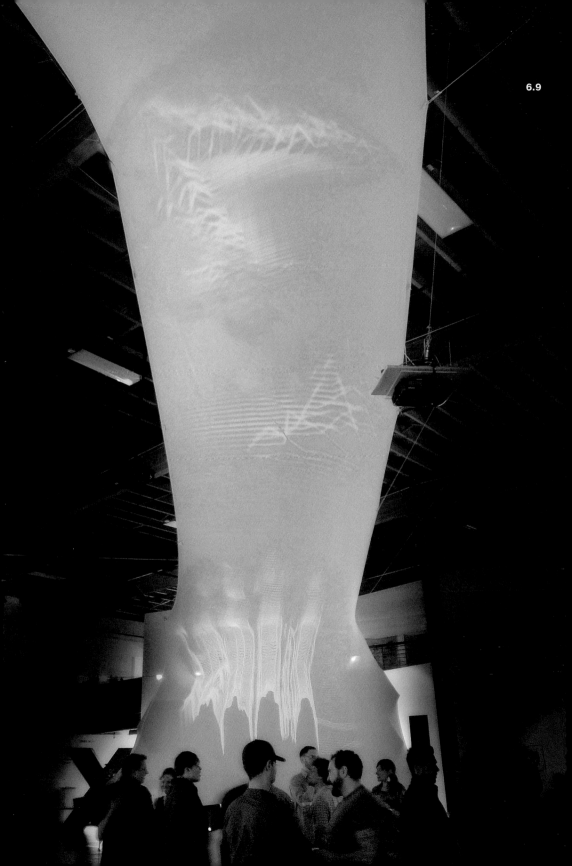

6.10

6.10—6.11
Brownsea Island Secret Safari
Revolting

Brownsea Island is a major attraction in Poole Harbour, UK. The island, now managed by the National Trust, was the birthplace of the Scout movement and is home to many rare animals.

Revolting art + design were commissioned to create a 'young people's alternative guide' to the island in order to encourage more young people to visit.

The island's unique habitat and rare flora and fauna inspired Revolting to create a 'secret safari'. The island was visited by a group of local school children who worked with the designers to create a number of fictitious animals they felt could inhabit it. The group examined the wildlife, terrain and many other factors and let this inform their ideas.

The creatures they came up with were then fleshed out by local illustrator Phil Smith and given a narrative by award-winning writer Joanna Quinn.

A digital installation was created that could be accessed via QR codes displayed around the site, allowing visitors to view these imaginative creations on their smartphones.

Well Done!
You've found a Squibideer!

I use my spooky eyes to hypnotise other creatures I don't like – and that includes humans – so I am not attacked or captured. I like my privacy. I live in a ditch and I am very

Sketching it out

A great test of an idea is to see if it can be recorded using a ballpoint pen and a napkin. If this is not possible, then the idea is probably too complicated.

A simple drawing is much quicker than a digital rendering and can communicate your idea with enough intent that you can judge its potential. Before sketching out ideas, it is useful to briefly think about what elements of the idea it is essential to communicate – is it the look, style, process, mechanics or application?

Each of these will require very different forms of notes and drawings and should be described in different ways. A sketch will emphasize the mass and dynamics of an object, and further notes can be used to describe ideas for the materials. If the drawing is trying to communicate use or mechanics it could show several different stages of a process with arrows and notes to describe the movement. Simple line drawings can describe the overall structure, but shading and cross-hatching can indicate mass, size and different surfaces.

Initial sketches often go a long way to explaining the thinking behind an idea at later stages. It is often a good idea to present a client with these concepts when you first meet them. When a person is faced with something final, their line of questioning will tend to focus on whether they like individual details, but when they see concept drawings they are more likely to talk about the idea itself.

6.12—6.15
TV criticism
Qian Lu (a student at Lyceé le Corbusier, France)

The beauty of sketching is that it allows you to explore concepts and ideas without any barriers or restrictions. These sketches explore our relationship with the ubiquitous medium of TV. They translate as, (6.12) People want to empty their mind; (6.13) We have the best French TV in the world; (6.14) We spend our tired time tied to this no-dignity box; (6.15) TV dulls educated people's minds and educates people living a dull life.

A drawing is simply a line going for a walk.

Paul Klee

6.12

Les gens veulent
se vider la tête

Julien Courbet

6.13

Nous avons la meilleure
télévision française du monde
Coluche

6.14

Nous surplombons cette boîte
qui n'a aucune dignité symbolique
et nous lui accordons
le temps fatigués de notre existence.

Fellini

6.15

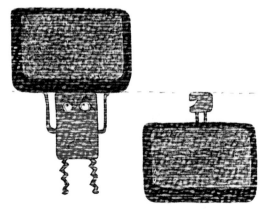

La télévision abrutit les gens cultivés
et cultive les gens qui mènent une vie abrutissante.

Umberto Eco

6.16—6.17

Mínimo Esfuerzo **magazine illustration**
Serse Rodríguez

For this special Edgar Allan Poe-inspired edition of *Minimo Esfuerzo* magazine, a range of Barcelona-based designers were selected to produce graphic responses to Poe's writing. In this illustration, Serse explores speculation about the author's drug and alcholol abuse, creating a dream-like result. Sketching and experimentation form a valid part of the exploration process.

6.17

6.16

6.18

6.18
Typography illustration
Karl Kwasny

A simple idea beautifully executed forms a strong, graphic
piece of communication. The craft of the design becomes a
crucial element for creating a brand and a point of difference.

Mood and concept boards

Mood and concept boards are essentially qualitative research methods that can be used to outline the expected attributes and benefits of an idea. They can be presented to clients to sum up large amounts of research and ideas.

A mood board will help visualize ideas in terms of colour palettes, textures and material choices; they are designed to give an overview of the elements that might go into an idea before concepts are ready to move forwards.

Concept boards usually consist of images mounted on large boards that demonstrate the idea in context. These would include images relating to the brand or client and their needs, as well as references to the ideal customer. These elements will be represented through collaged imagery, but this can be supported by key terms and factual information gathered through research.

A concept board can also demonstrate broad context by placing the product or service up against its competitors. This will show how others have approached similar problems and the tone of voice they have used, providing a benchmark for your ideas to be judged against.

6.19—6.21
Wallspace
Salad Creative

Wallspace create easy-to-use, digitally printed vinyl that can be applied to different wall surfaces. Salad Creative designed an innovative, adaptable and versatile identity for Wallspace that works with a range of colours and arrangements on various types of media.

6.19

6.20

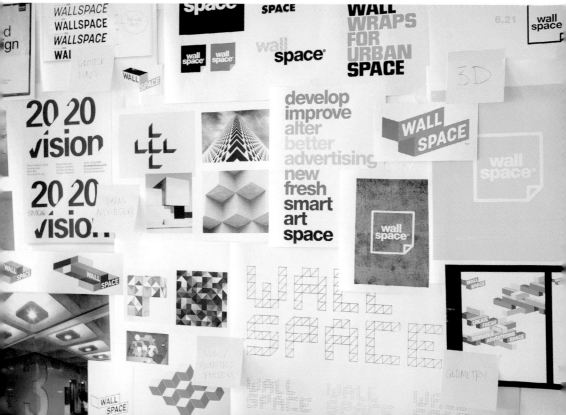

6.21

Rationale

Knowing why particular choices have been made will help you to explain their value. Having a clear rationale for each of your decisions will demonstrate the soundness of the choice and the strength of the knowledge that informed them. A good presentation should start with an overview of the process that has led to the idea presented, and it is important to have a clear and thorough rationale for each of the stages shown to the client.

Following these steps will help you to communicate the rationale behind your ideas effectively and persuasively:

1 Reiterate the brief and the key objectives of the project.

2 Detail the key areas of development and tell the client what processes you have applied.

3 Be clear and concise – you do not have to show the client everything, but have all pertinent information close to hand.

4 Make notes, as it is easy to forget key points – bullet points are often best.

5 Rehearse the presentation to ensure clarity, even if it is just spoken aloud to yourself – this can help you get the rhythm right and iron out any kinks.

6 Remember, there is a reason you followed the path travelled, so take the client on the same journey and make it obvious there was only one clear destination.

6.22
Natural History Museum Discovery Guides
Hat-trick Design

This series of guides was produced to meet a very specific brief, as Jim Sutherland of Hat-trick Design explains: 'The Natural History Museum wanted to produce school materials that made learning about nature engaging, open, accessible and fun, to reflect the core values of the museum itself. The solution was to create covers for the guides that the children could play and interact with, to bring the animals and galleries to life. These were perforated so they could be torn off once the activities were completed and kept by the children at school or at home, getting the brand to live outside of the museum itself.'

We wanted the children to have something to tear off and keep. In the past you filled in the papers and gave them back, there was no interaction, nothing to remember or keep hold of.

Jim Sutherland, Hat-trick Design

NATURAL
HISTORY
MUSEUM

Explore and Discover...
Animal parts
the animal adventure

6.23

6.23—6.24

Natural History Museum Discovery Guides
Hat-trick Design

The resulting guides encourage interactivity and create a memorable and imaginative set of learning materials. This creativity captures the imagination of children, making learning a fun activity.

Once a client is ready to move forward with an idea, the next step is making it work. Often the most challenging part of the idea generation process is realizing the outcomes. This will inevitably present many unexpected challenges that will require further searching for solutions.

Many ideas are rethought as rendering starts to take place and problems are encountered, and at this point investigation and testing is needed in order to complete the process.

Back to the design brief

Once ideas are finalized, re-interrogate the initial brief and check that all of the objectives have been met. Inevitably projects will evolve once idea generation and research processes are employed, but the client will need to be kept up to date with any major changes if the project has moved on significantly from their original requests.

Idea generation often reveals ways of enhancing and promoting the product or service that go beyond the brief and the process will lead you to unexpected places. If the designs veer away from the requirements of the brief it is usually because testing of ideas through research has proven there are more vital concerns, or better ways of presenting the necessary information.

Most importantly, you must deliver on the brief in a way that can be approved and used by the client; even if this delivery is made in unusual or unexpected ways. Keeping in touch with the client will allow for a partnership that pushes the brief to its limits, and also allow for growth and long-lasting and productive working relationships.

Logos and logotypes
A logo is a graphic symbol that represents a brand, business or organization. It can be an abstract symbol or an icon reflecting the nature of the business. A logotype incorporates the name of the organization into the icon.

Considering the target audience

After reconsidering the brief, it is wise to check ideas with the target audience. This can be approached in a number of ways; ideas can be tested through focus groups and questionnaires, or prototypes can be built for evaluation.

Focus groups are a good way to gauge the opinions of people and create debate – they can also lead to new lines of enquiry. The most productive way to run a focus group is to select a varied cross-section of the identified audience (not just your friends and colleagues) and to set themes for discussion. There should be a chair to monitor the conversation and ensure that all of the necessary points are discussed, but the conversation can be allowed to go off-track as sometimes this will lead to new ideas. Recording the conversation is vital as referencing it afterwards can be difficult without a record of what was said.

Outside of talking to the target group, following up-to-date market research and examining current trends and styles will help focus concepts. This information can be gathered in a number of ways; there are specific trendspotting websites and journals, or the design team can simply investigate and report back on what they see, in order to build a picture of what the audience is currently favouring, within the area being designed for.

6.25

6.25—6.26
William Patten Primary School
Planning Unit

This <u>logo</u> (6.25) and <u>logotype</u> (6.26) combine the letterforms to visually describe the school they were designed for. They both give an immediate sense of inclusion, care and protection.

6.26

William Patten
Primary School

Testing solutions

Testing will help you gain the insight needed to ensure that your ideas are workable. There are many ways to test a concept, from audience and viability tests to materials and mechanics, and there are several points at which these tests should be conducted. Firstly, solutions will be tested against the brief, key audience representatives and the client – ideas that are thought to be viable will then proceed to design development and further stages of testing.

Usability tests will quickly reveal whether or not a solution is fit for purpose. They look to prove usability, durability and highlight any potential problems. Usability tests can involve giving the audience a physical prototype to use for a specified amount of time – they will simply be asked to use it and see what happens. They can also be used to test the audience's capacity to use non-tactile items, such as banking interfaces, websites and online ordering services.

This is a crucial point in the design cycle as it will prove either that your ideas have paid off, that they need further development, or perhaps even suggest uses and possibilities that you had not considered. This should be monitored, and the candidates interviewed after the tests to gain further insight.

The key to successful idea generation is to ensure that no design decision is arbitrary, that every section has been thought through and that there is a narrative – this is often the most convincing argument that can be made. However, even a narrative must be backed up with numbers and provable results gained through research and testing – these will prove beyond doubt that the right choices were made.

6.27

Why test?

You test projects because, in most cases, you are not a member of the intended audience and therefore must find a way of understanding the needs of the end-user. By testing your ideas on members of the intended audience you can quickly gather a lot of pertinent information that will help you make relevant and informed choices.

Tip #21 – Be prepared

Always carry something to make notes with. Smartphones can be a designer's best friend as they allow you to capture images, film and sound as well as applications that help you to record and categorize inspiration on the move.

6.27

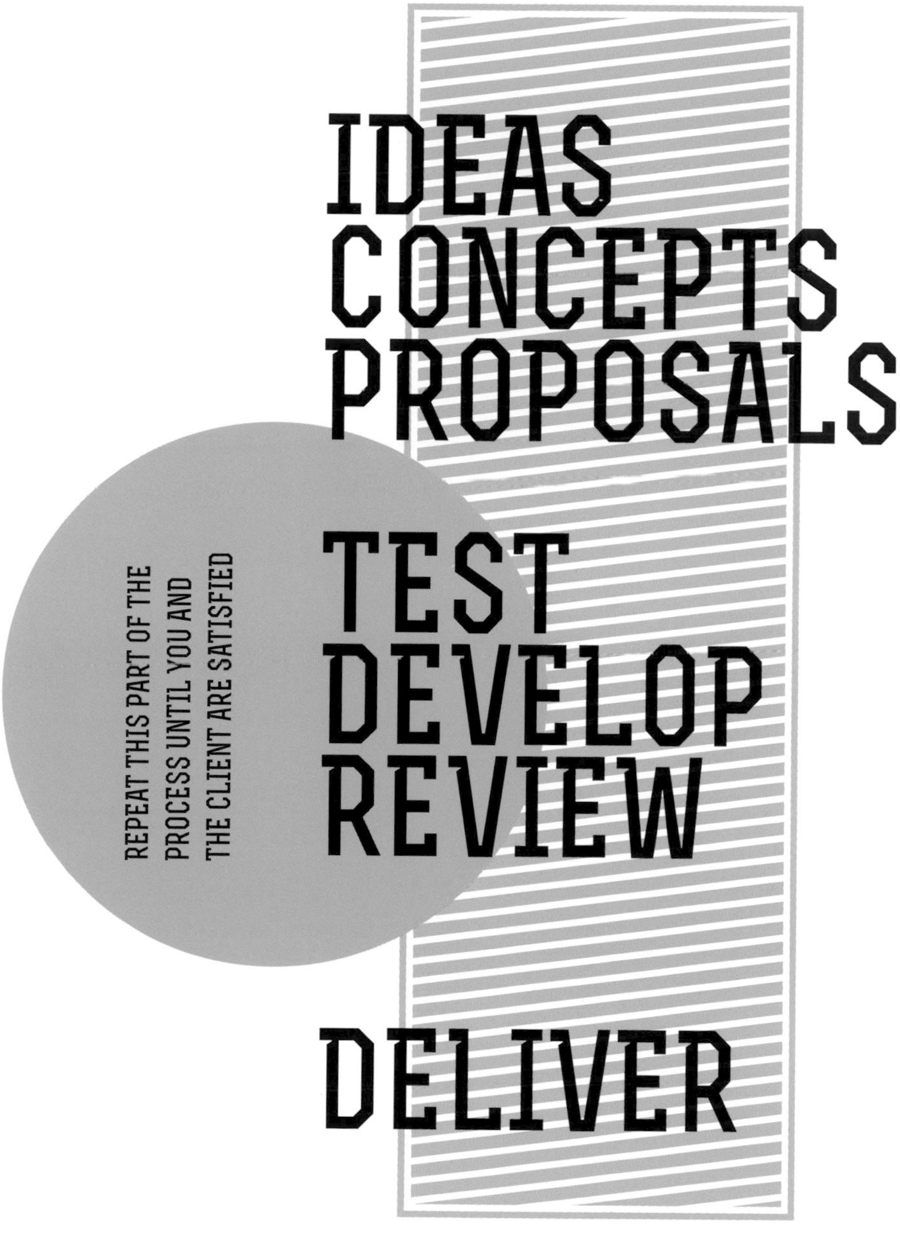

IDEAS
CONCEPTS
PROPOSALS

TEST
DEVELOP
REVIEW

REPEAT THIS PART OF THE
PROCESS UNTIL YOU AND
THE CLIENT ARE SATISFIED

DELIVER

Studio interview:

Salad Creative

Andy Russell is head of design at Salad Creative and has worked with clients such as Animal, Beaujais, Johnson & Johnson, Lush, Maximuscle, Mubadala, Myla, P&O Cruises, Red Bull Racing, Salomon, and Yell Group.

Are there any processes you have developed to help kick-start the idea generation process?

I usually start by looking through old sketchbooks or 'inspiration' folders from previous projects. This is for two reasons: firstly, a lot of the time clients will come to us with a different brief for the same problem. Secondly, we are all guilty of looking to other designers for the answers, when we have access to a vault of unused ideas of our own.

How do your best ideas occur?

I tend to think better when I'm under pressure, when I have less time to over-think a problem. It's not my preferred method of working and isn't good for the stress levels, but it has produced some successful results.

Having said that, switching off and 'forgetting about it' can be just as conducive.

When do you know you have the 'golden idea'?

They can vary from project to project but the truth is you never truly know if you have a 'golden idea'. Generally, gut instinct is a good indicator and if something feels right, then go with it. This works for most things in life.

What are the most effective ways to communicate your ideas?

Talking is always a good start, but so is listening. It's much easier to communicate your ideas if you take the time to listen first. That way you won't trip yourself up when it comes to rationalizing concepts or selling an idea.

I also like to present my work in a logical manner. Start at the beginning and take whoever I'm talking to through the process. It helps them understand the logic behind the madness.

Do you ever have creative blocks, and if so, how do you overcome them?

Always. Creativity or being creative is not something that you can just switch on. It's a kind of subconscious that can be, on occasions, a little temperamental. I have yet to find a guaranteed fix, but getting away from my desk is normally the first thing I try. That and just having lunch helps.

The working environment can inform and accelerate the creative process. There is no substitute for being able to print, review, pin-up and rearrange pieces of work.

Presenting and categorizing ideas

To help you present your ideas to your clients as visuals, you are asked to create a typology in the form of a board, similar to a mood board, but concentrating on a specific theme. This will help you categorize your ideas and findings.

Brief

Select one aspect of packaging and find several different examples of it. You may, for instance, pick bottle tops, washing powder boxes, or perfume cases. It is best if you can photograph the collected elements, so you have more control over how they are displayed and can give them equal presence.

From here you can begin to decide how you will categorize the elements and which you will highlight. You may wish to display them according to colour, shape, size, logotypes or typography.

This will help you establish the most popular choices and designs within a particular range of products. The information gained during this exercise can be useful when you need to visually prove to a client that your work fits within a genre, or challenges it.

Project objectives

- To help develop your ability to present, categorize and identify trends in design.

Recommended reading related to this project

Ambrose, G and Harris, P (2008). *The Fundamentals of Graphic Design.* AVA Publishing

Elam, K (2011). *Geometry of Design: Studies in Proportion and Composition.* Princeton Architectural Press

Elam, K (2004). *Grid Systems: Principles of Organizing Type (Design Briefs).* Princeton Architectural Press

Macnab, M (2008). *Decoding Design: Understanding and Using Symbols in Visual Communication.* How Design Books

Noble, I and Bestley, R (2011). *Visual Research: An Introduction to Research Methodologies in Graphic Design.* AVA Publishing; Second Edition

Wigan, M (2006). *Basics Illustration: Thinking Visually.* AVA Publishing

Conclusion

The best design relies heavily on focused and appropriate ideas – no matter what level of skill you have, if your idea falls flat, the project will almost certainly follow.

Great ideas come from knowledge, experimentation and perseverance, and after reading this book you will be armed with the skills needed to succeed. Whether you are working alone or in a team you will be able to employ one of the many devices offered as a way of generating purposeful ideas.

Often strong ideas can be hard to come by, but just as an athlete trains their body, the mind can be trained to arrive quickly at creative solutions to problems. This book has explained some of the many processes you can use to enhance idea generation activities. All of these methods should be fun and engaging, allowing you to reach successful conclusions.

Each project and good idea will lead to another. Once you find the activity that works best, you should research it further. Each of the notable theorists and designers mentioned in this text have much more to say, and reading their work will help you develop further as a designer.

This book is the beginning of your journey as an informed and active thinker who can achieve ideas beyond those arrived at by flicking through the latest design periodicals – you will be out there observing, recording, documenting and talking to people.

You will be informed and ready to seize inspiration.

Contributor contacts

Albers, J *(2006). Interaction of Color*. Yale University Press

Ambrose, G and Harris, P (2007). *Basics Design 05: Colour*. AVA Publishing

Ambrose, G and Harris, P (2008). *The Fundamentals of Graphic Design*. AVA Publishing

Arden, P (2003). *It's Not How Good You Are, It's How Good You Want To Be*. Phaidon Press

Armstrong, H (2009). *Graphic Design Theory: Readings from the Field*. Princeton Architectural Press

Baldwin, J and Roberts, L (2006). *Visual Communication: From Theory to Practice*. AVA Publishing

Barry, P (2008). *The Advertising Concept Book: Think Now, Design Later*. Thames & Hudson

Barthes, R (author) and Lavers, A (translator) (2009). *Mythologies*. Vintage Classics

Bayley, S (1992). *Taste: The Secret Meaning of Things*. Pantheon Books Inc.

Berger, J (2009). *About Looking*. Bloomsbury Publishing Plc.

Burtenshaw, K et al (2011). *The Fundamentals of Creative Advertising*. AVA Publishing; second edition

Chandler, D (2007). *Semiotics: The Basics*. Routledge

Clarke, M (2007). *Verbalising the Visual: Translating Art and Design into Words*. AVA Publishing

Cullen, K (2007). *Layout Workbook: A Real-world Guide to Building Pages in Graphic Design*. Rockport Publishers Inc.

de Bono, E (2009). *Six Thinking Hats*. Penguin

Debord, G (1984). *Society of the Spectacle*. Black & Red, US

Elam, K (2001). *Geometry of Design: Studies in Proportion and Composition (Design Briefs)*. Princeton Architectural Press

Elam, K (2004). *Grid Systems: Principles of Organizing Type (Design Briefs)*. Princeton Architectural Press

Eskilson, S (2007). *Graphic Design: A New History*. Laurence King

Evamy, M (2007). *Logo*. Laurence King

Foster, J (2003). *How to Get Ideas*. Berrett-Koehler; First edition

Gatter, G (2010). *Production for Print*. Laurence King; 2nd revised edition

Heller, S and Vienne, V (2012). *100 Ideas that Changed Graphic Design*. Laurence King

Heller, S and Talarico, L (2010). *Graphic: Inside the Sketchbooks of the World's Great Graphic Designers*. Thames & Hudson

Heller, S and Talarico, L (2011). *Typography Sketchbooks*. Thames & Hudson

Knight, C and Glaser, J (2010). *The Graphic Design Exercise Book*. RotoVision

Kress, G and Van Leeuwen, T (1996). *Reading Images: The Grammar of Visual Design*. Routledge

Lupton, E & Miller, J (1993). *The ABCs of the Bauhaus: The Bauhaus and Design Theory*. Thames & Hudson

Lupton, E (2008). *Area_2*. Phaidon Press Ltd

Lupton, E and Abbott Miller, J (1999). *Design Writing Research*. Phaidon Press

Marshall, L and Meachem, L (2012). *How to Use Type*. Laurence King

Morioka, A (2008). *Color Design Workbook: A Real World Guide to Using Color in Graphic Design*. Rockport Publishers Inc.

Olins, W (2008). *Wally Olins: The Brand Handbook*. Thames & Hudson; 1st edition

Poynor, R. (2003). *No more rules: Graphic Design and Postmodernism*. Laurence King

Roberts, L (2006). *GOOD: An Introduction to Ethics in Graphic Design*. AVA Publishing

Sawyer, R (2012). *Explaining Creativity: The Science of Human Innovation*. OUP USA; 2nd edition

Schenck, E (2006). *The Houdini Solution: Why Thinking Inside the Box is the Key to Creativity*. McGraw-Hill Contemporary

Squire, V (2006). *Getting it Right with Type: The Do's and Don'ts of Typography*. Laurence King

Stone, T (2010). *Managing the Design Process, Volume 1: Concept Development*. Rockport Publishing Inc.

Viction:ary (2009). *Colour Mania*. Viction Workshop Ltd; 4th edition

Wheeler, A (2009). *Designing Brand Identity: An Essential Guide for the Whole Branding Team*. John Wiley & Sons; 3rd edition

Index

Page numbers in *italics* denote illustration captions.

Acknowledgements

Thank you to Sarah, Mary, Phil and Rachel Leonard, Katie and Manuel Cruz, Anna Middleton, Paul Allen, Neil Mabbs, Jacqui Sayers, Sarah Turner, Gavin Ambrose, Kit Johnson and all of the students I have worked with who inspired this book.

The publisher would like to thank Barrie Tullett and Graham Jones for their comments on the manuscript.

Image credits:

Cover image by Vesna Pešić BECHA and Sushi.

Page 3, 12–13, 58–59, 92–93: Images courtesy of Dowling Duncan.

Pages 7, 34–37, 80–81, 86–87, 114–117: Images courtesy of The Creative Method.

Pages 11, 39, 158–161, 174–177: Images courtesy of Hat-trick Design Consultants Ltd.

Pages 14–15: Images courtesy of Studio Myerscough.

Pages 16–17: Box set designed by Webb & Webb Design Ltd.

Harry Potter and the Prisoner of Azkaban: Cover and endpaper illustrations by Clare Melinsky 2010, © J.K. Rowling 1999, reproduced by permission of The Blair Agency and Bloomsbury Publishing Plc. Harry Potter and the Goblet of Fire: Cover and endpaper illustrations by Clare Melinsky 2010, © J.K. Rowling 2000, reproduced by permission of The Blair Agency and Bloomsbury Publishing Plc.

Harry Potter and the Half Blood Prince: Cover and endpaper illustrations by Clare Melinsky 2010, © J.K. Rowling 2005, reproduced by permission of The Blair Agency and Bloomsbury Publishing Plc.

Pages 18–19: Images courtesy of Vesna Pešic BECHA and Sushi.

Pages 20–21: Images courtesy of Peter Gregson Studio.

Pages 25, 179: Images courtesy of Planning Unit.

Pages 26–27, 108–109, 152–153: Images courtesy of re-shape invent.

Pages 31, 111: Images courtesy of Reform Creative Ltd.

Pages 32–33, 98–99: Images courtesy of Karoshi.

Pages 44–47, 72–73, 75: Images courtesy of Sam Winston.

Page 49: Image copyright Andy Vella.

Pages 50–51: Images courtesy of Matthieu Delahaie.

Page 53: Images courtesy of Tanner Christensen.

Pages 56–57, 95–97: Images courtesy of Happy F&B.

Pages 60–61: Images courtesy of Daye Kim Design.

Pages 62–63: Images courtesy of Social.

Page 65: Image courtesy of Dover Publications.

Pages 66–67, 169: Images courtesy of Qian Lu.

Page 69: Image courtesy of Adbusters.org

Page 71: Images courtesy and copyright of Andy Vella and Bloomsbury Publishing Plc.

Page 83: Image courtesy of Shutterstock.com and © Chris Loneragan.

Pages 85, 128–131: Images courtesy of Haime & Butler.

Pages 88–89: Images courtesy of Voice.

Pages 102–103: Images courtesy of Catherine Griffiths.

Pages 112–113: Images courtesy of Thames & Hudson Ltd and Grade Design.

Pages 118–119: Images courtesy of James Kape and Briton Smith.

Pages 122–123, 139, 143: Images courtesy of Nikola Arežina.

Page 133: Images courtesy of James Kape.

Pages 144–147: Images courtesy of Webb & Webb Design Ltd.

Pages 149–151, 172–173, 183: Images courtesy of Salad Creative.

Pages 164–165: Images courtesy of Second Story.

Pages 166–167: Images courtesy of Revolting.

Page 170: Images courtesy of Serse Rodríguez.

Page 171: Illustration courtesy of Karl Kwasny.

All reasonable attempts have been made to trace, clear and credit the copyright holders of the images reproduced in this book. However, if any credits have been inadvertently omitted, the publisher will endeavour to incorporate amendments in future editions.

Publisher's note

The subject of ethics is not new, yet its consideration within the applied visual arts is perhaps not as prevalent as it might be. Our aim here is to help a new generation of students, educators and practitioners find a methodology for structuring their thoughts and reflections in this vital area.

AVA Publishing hopes that these **Working with ethics** pages provide a platform for consideration and a flexible method for incorporating ethical concerns in the work of educators, students and professionals. Our approach consists of four parts:

The **introduction** is intended to be an accessible snapshot of the ethical landscape, both in terms of historical development and current dominant themes.

The **framework** positions ethical consideration into four areas and poses questions about the practical implications that might occur. Marking your response to each of these questions on the scale shown will allow your reactions to be further explored by comparison.

The **case study** sets out a real project and then poses some ethical questions for further consideration. This is a focus point for a debate rather than a critical analysis so there are no predetermined right or wrong answers.

A selection of **further reading** for you to consider areas of particular interest in more detail.

Ethical: aware-
ness/
reflect-
ion/
debate

Working with ethics

Introduction

Ethics is a complex subject that interlaces the idea of responsibilities to society with a wide range of considerations relevant to the character and happiness of the individual. It concerns virtues of compassion, loyalty and strength, but also of confidence, imagination, humour and optimism. As introduced in ancient Greek philosophy, the fundamental ethical question is: *what should I do?* How we might pursue a 'good' life not only raises moral concerns about the effects of our actions on others, but also personal concerns about our own integrity.

In modern times the most important and controversial questions in ethics have been the moral ones. With growing populations and improvements in mobility and communications, it is not surprising that considerations about how to structure our lives together on the planet should come to the forefront. For visual artists and communicators, it should be no surprise that these considerations will enter into the creative process.

Some ethical considerations are already enshrined in government laws and regulations or in professional codes of conduct. For example, plagiarism and breaches of confidentiality can be punishable offences. Legislation in various nations makes it unlawful to exclude people with disabilities from accessing information or spaces. The trade of ivory as a material has been banned in many countries. In these cases, a clear line has been drawn under what is unacceptable.

But most ethical matters remain open to debate, among experts and lay-people alike, and in the end we have to make our own choices on the basis of our own guiding principles or values. Is it more ethical to work for a charity than for a commercial company? Is it unethical to create something that others find ugly or offensive?

Specific questions such as these may lead to other questions that are more abstract. For example, is it only effects on humans (and what they care about) that are important, or might effects on the natural world require attention too?

Is promoting ethical consequences justified even when it requires ethical sacrifices along the way? Must there be a single unifying theory of ethics (such as the Utilitarian thesis that the right course of action is always the one that leads to the greatest happiness of the greatest number), or might there always be many different ethical values that pull a person in various directions?

As we enter into ethical debate and engage with these dilemmas on a personal and professional level, we may change our views or change our view of others. The real test though is whether, as we reflect on these matters, we change the way we act as well as the way we think. Socrates, the 'father' of philosophy, proposed that people will naturally do 'good' if they know what is right. But this point might only lead us to yet another question: *how do we know what is right?*

You
What are your ethical beliefs?

Central to everything you do will be your attitude to people and issues around you. For some people, their ethics are an active part of the decisions they make every day as a consumer, a voter or a working professional. Others may think about ethics very little and yet this does not automatically make them unethical. Personal beliefs, lifestyle, politics, nationality, religion, gender, class or education can all influence your ethical viewpoint.

Using the scale, where would you place yourself? What do you take into account to make your decision? Compare results with your friends or colleagues.

Your client
What are your terms?

Working relationships are central to whether ethics can be embedded into a project, and your conduct on a day-to-day basis is a demonstration of your professional ethics. The decision with the biggest impact is whom you choose to work with in the first place. Cigarette companies or arms traders are often-cited examples when talking about where a line might be drawn, but rarely are real situations so extreme. At what point might you turn down a project on ethical grounds and how much does the reality of having to earn a living affect your ability to choose?

Using the scale, where would you place a project? How does this compare to your personal ethical level?

01 02 03 04 05 06 07 08 09 10

01 02 03 04 05 06 07 08 09 10

Your specifications
What are the impacts of your materials?

In relatively recent times, we are learning that many natural materials are in short supply. At the same time, we are increasingly aware that some man-made materials can have harmful, long-term effects on people or the planet. How much do you know about the materials that you use? Do you know where they come from, how far they travel and under what conditions they are obtained? When your creation is no longer needed, will it be easy and safe to recycle? Will it disappear without a trace? Are these considerations your responsibility or are they out of your hands?

Using the scale, mark how ethical your material choices are.

Your creation
What is the purpose of your work?

Between you, your colleagues and an agreed brief, what will your creation achieve? What purpose will it have in society and will it make a positive contribution? Should your work result in more than commercial success or industry awards? Might your creation help save lives, educate, protect or inspire? Form and function are two established aspects of judging a creation, but there is little consensus on the obligations of visual artists and communicators toward society, or the role they might have in solving social or environmental problems. If you want recognition for being the creator, how responsible are you for what you create and where might that responsibility end?

Using the scale, mark how ethical the purpose of your work is.

01 02 03 04 05 06 07 08 09 10

01 02 03 04 05 06 07 08 09 10

Working with ethics

One aspect of graphic design that raises an ethical dilemma is that of its relationship with the creation of printed materials and the environmental impacts of print production. For example, in the UK, it is estimated that around 5.4 billion items of addressed direct mail are sent out every year and these, along with other promotional inserts, amount to over half a million tonnes of paper annually (almost 5 per cent of the UK consumption of paper and board). Response rates to mail campaigns are known to be between 1–3 per cent, making junk mail arguably one of the least environmentally friendly forms of print communication. As well as the use of paper or board, the design decisions to use scratch-off panels, heavily coated gloss finishes, full-colour ink-intensive graphics or glues for seals or fixings make paper more difficult to recycle once it has been discarded. How much responsibility should a graphic designer have in this situation if a client has already chosen to embark on a direct mail campaign and has a format in mind? Even if designers wish to minimise the environmental impacts of print materials, what might they most usefully do?

In 1951, Leo Burnett (the famous advertising executive known for creating the Jolly Green Giant and the Marlboro Man) was hired to create a campaign for Kellogg's new cereal, Sugar Frosted Flakes (now Frosties in the UK and Frosted Flakes in the US). Tony the Tiger, designed by children's book illustrator Martin Provensen, was one of four characters selected to sell the cereal. Newt the Gnu and Elmo the Elephant never made it to the shelves and after Tony proved more popular than Katy the Kangaroo, she was dropped from packs after the first year.

Whilst the orange-and-black tiger stripes and the red kerchief have remained, Provensen's original design for Tony has changed significantly since he first appeared in 1952. Tony started out with an American football-shaped head, which later became more rounded, and his eye colour changed from green to gold. Today, his head is more angular and he sits on a predominantly blue background. Tony was initially presented as a character that walked on all fours and was no bigger than a cereal box. By the 1970s, Tony's physique had developed into a slim and muscular six-foot-tall standing figure.

Between 1952 and 1995 Kellogg's are said to have spent more than USD$1 billion promoting Frosted Flakes with Tony's image, while generating USD$5.3 billion in gross US sales. But surveys by consumer rights groups such as Which? find that over 75 per cent of people believe that using characters on packaging makes it hard for parents to say no to their children. In these surveys, Kellogg's come under specific scrutiny for Frosties, which are said to contain one third sugar and more salt than the Food Standards Agency recommends. In response, Kellogg's have said: 'We are committed to responsibly marketing our brands and communicating their intrinsic qualities so that our customers can make informed choices.'

Food campaigners claim that the use of cartoon characters is a particularly manipulative part of the problem and governments should stop them being used on less healthy children's foods. But in 2008, spokespeople for the Food and Drink Federation in the UK, said: 'We are baffled as to why Which? wants to take all the fun out of food by banning popular brand characters, many of whom have been adding colour to supermarket shelves for more than 80 years.'

Is it more ethical to create promotional graphics for 'healthy' rather than 'unhealthy' food products?

Is it unethical to design cartoon characters to appeal to children for commercial purposes?

Would you have worked on this project, either now or in the 1950s?

I studied graphic design in Germany, and my professor emphasised the responsibility that designers and illustrators have towards the people they create things for.

Eric Carle (illustrator)

AIGA
Design Business and Ethics
2007, AIGA

Eaton, Marcia Muelder
Aesthetics and the Good Life
1989, Associated University Press

Ellison, David
Ethics and Aesthetics in European Modernist Literature:
From the Sublime to the Uncanny
2001, Cambridge University Press

Fenner, David E W (Ed)
Ethics and the Arts:
An Anthology
1995, Garland Reference Library of Social Science

Gini, Al and Marcoux, Alexei M
Case Studies in Business Ethics
2005, Prentice Hall

McDonough, William and Braungart, Michael
Cradle to Cradle:
Remaking the Way We Make Things
2002, North Point Press

Papanek, Victor
Design for the Real World:
Making to Measure
1972, Thames & Hudson

United Nations Global Compact
The Ten Principles
www.unglobalcompact.org/AboutTheGC/TheTenPrinciples/index.html